THE DISHWASHER DIALOGUES

THE DISHWASHER DIALOGUES

Gregory James Light
and
Rafael Sinclair Mahdavi

Printed and published by
Orléans Press

ISBN 9782956249122

To the Memory of
Leroy Haynes

Table of Contents

Preface

Our book resembles a *cadavre exquis*, a French term invented in 1925 by the Surrealists describing a game played by two or more people creating a mutual composition. The first player draws an image or writes a phrase on a blank sheet of paper. Then folds the paper. The next player adds to the story or image after seeing only a fragment of the previous contribution. And so on and so forth, like these dialogues, which, when unfolded and read, reveal our story. Our *cadavre exquis* is set in nineteen-seventies Paris, when we worked for Leroy Haynes in his legendary American soul food restaurant, *Chez Haynes*, near Pigalle.

We talked about this project for many years, almost since the day that era came to an end. Year after year, then decade by decade, we came back to thinking about those days and, somehow, chronicling them. Our memories were shuffled away, then brought out and dusted off, then shelved once more. We met in London on several occasions and talked and visited museums and art galleries. And talked some more.

Then, in 2020, the global Covid-19 Pandemic arrived and is still killing as of this writing. Restrictions restricted. Lockdowns locked down. For the first six months, it looked like it would not be that bad. The hard autumn came, and the memories of Leroy and *Chez Haynes* and those years came back with more urgency. The memories began to stick. No excuses left. The fickleness of time was suddenly evident. We had to write about the *Chez Haynes* years. Crazy, intense, creative, thriving on freedom and a *carte orange*. We plunged in. Always aware that, as that mother of all gossipers Marcel Proust said, remembrance of things past isn't always of things as they were.

Of course. What else would you expect? Certainly not precise dialogue or exact descriptions. But close enough.

Enough to start. An email exchange began between us, between two islands: one of us on the Greek island of Paros and the other on Miramichi Island north of Toronto. Start writing, and I will cut in, one of us said. Our brains assured us there were more of these unknown knowns just over the memory horizon. We'd splice our writing into a dialogue, trusting the exchange and a font change would preserve our different voices as they were back then, and continue in some form today. Sometimes successfully. Sometimes less so … well, you dear reader, be the judge.

This project would morph into stories and conversations about nostalgia, melancholia, women, friendship, art, death, comedy, and more. We refer to our exchanges as *the dishwasher dialogues* after our work at *Chez Haynes*. We met in Paris exactly a year after we started this *cadavre exquis*. To conclude it. We walked, talked, refreshed our memories and, of course, brought many more memories back from the dead. But those will have to wait for another day.

That is how this book started. And was completed.

The seventies were a surreal, exhilarating decade in Paris; it was a city still reeling from the social upheaval of the sixties. We belonged to a self-confident generation; everything was possible in our lives, and we lived under the radar, or to be honest, we survived illegally. Nobody asked us for working or residence papers, and if the police stopped us in the metro, we just told them we were on our way to Belgium, Italy, England, or Spain, and they let us go.

We were undoubtedly lucky our youth came at that time. Paris was synonymous with freedom, then. Even the Parisians' irritated gestures and comments about the smallest request or interaction—touching a pear for ripeness in a market, refusing to change a five-franc coin—was like a breath of fresh air: any behavior was permissible because all behavior was somehow incorrect. But it wasn't regulated. Those were the days when a student visa or *carte de séjour* was an accessory, not an obligation. Jobs and rooms came and went. Travel in Paris was essentially free. And you could get a full Chinese meal next to the metro Odéon for five francs. In 1975 five French francs were roughly worth one dollar.

A final note: In these dialogues, we unashamedly drop names of the eminent, famous, and once-famous. It is not profuse, but it is overt. It is not to decorate or impress. At least not all the time. These people were there and carried celebrity and, therefore, curiosity. While we have no embarrassment about identifying them, neither do we reveal anything shockingly, or even tediously, new about them. Be assured we have forgotten many brushes with celebrity, and to those who are missing from our reminiscences, we apologize. Not that they would ever know.

Our more fascinating friends and comrades, who shared these times and events with us—often exhaustively and intimately—we have left respectfully unidentified. When that was not possible, we used pseudonyms. They know who they are. We hope we have given them plausible deniability. Besides, they know the truth. And accuracy and veracity have a nasty habit of meddling with story and memory. To them, we owe the best of times and a share of the worst of times. It is also to them we dedicate this book.

Gregory James Light
Rafael Sinclair Mahdavi

Paris November 2021

Note to Reader

The change in the two authors' voices in the dialogues is indicated by a change in font.

1.

Le patron de Chez Haynes

I LEFT MANHATTAN BECAUSE I missed Europe. I was a US citizen then, Greg, and still am, but have since acquired a few more passports, three more to be exact. I feel safer that way now. No country is going to fuck with me in the name of patriotism. I alone will decide for what or whom I am willing to die. I flew to Paris because I had been there in the late sixties. I had fled the U.S. to avoid the draft and being sent to the war in Vietnam. By this time, in late 1975, I had been amnestied, and I stayed with friends in the Latin Quarter. There was a young woman also staying there who told me there might be a job opening at a place called *Chez Haynes*, up in Pigalle, off the Rue des Martyrs. The restaurant was a legendary hangout, owned and run by Leroy Haynes, himself a legendary African American, one of the first in U.S. Army Intelligence, who had fought at Guadalcanal in the Pacific. Later, stationed in Berlin, Leroy learned about the upcoming U.S. Army deployment to Korea and resigned his commission. He went to Paris with his friend Don and started cooking and selling southern, honey-fried chicken from a pushcart in the streets of Pigalle.

My road to *Chez Haynes* restaurant and to Leroy was the same road that led to my first meeting you, Rafael. February 1976. For me, that road started on a Stretched-DC8 from New York to Luxembourg. Air Icelandic. A return ticket to Europe for $190. I never used the return portion. On the plane, I met Harry who was sitting in the seat next to me. He was young, even younger than me (I was only 24), and from somewhere on the west coast. Great guy, funny and open to just about everything. We parted in Luxembourg. He was 'doing Europe'. I was going on to Paris having 'done Europe' four years earlier. But he had a cousin, Wendy, in Paris. He gave me her address and said he'd be there soon. With the best of intentions, we said we'd get in touch when he got to Paris, but I lost his cousin's address on the train to Paris. As fate (or whatever stood in for the Parisian gods in February 1976) would have it, I bumped into him a week or so later, on Boulevard St. Germain, around the corner from a cheap hotel I had booked into on Rue Saint André des Arts, in the Latin Quarter. He was with Wendy. They were going up north to an American soul food restaurant where she worked as a waitress. So, I tagged along. And *voilà*! Leroy, you and what would become a four-year adventure.

I never found out how or why, but Leroy knew a lot of people. He knew the local cops, gave them free meals and free booze once in a while. Sometimes he made out bogus restaurant bills for them so they could make a bit extra on the side by getting reimbursed for meals they never had. Leroy also knew French film stars like Jean-Paul Belmondo. The mayor of Paris, Jacques Chirac, was also a buddy of Leroy's. Chirac often gave his press conferences at *Chez Haynes*. And there were the shady characters from the racetracks too, they dropped by and gave Leroy hot tips on the hot horses. Flower sellers came by as well. They never declared their income but informed the police who was where and when in the restaurants in Pigalle at night. So, the cops left the flower sellers alone. One of them was a young Sicilian named Liliana. I asked her out when she came by one evening. The next day, three heavy-set dudes came in and asked me if I was planning to marry their sister Liliana. I said no. 'Then stay away and keep your hands off her or else we'll be back'. I said '*bien sûr, pas de problème*'. That's the way it was. Leroy didn't give a shit if his staff was legal or had residence papers or work permits. Over the years I've come to suspect that from his army intelligence days, Leroy had built a formidable network of acquaintances, from the U.S. embassy down to the Parisian cops on the beat.

And thank God for that. I don't know how many of his friends and connections in the Parisian political and cultural hierarchy looked the other way, or if that was just the way it was, but it saved me from the imminent threat of hunger tapping me on the shoulder. I needed that job. Work permits never crossed my mind for the first two years I lived in Paris. To tell you the truth, they were far above my pay grade, which admittedly was non-existent. I repeat, I needed that job. My first and only other job, as a live-out au pair for a two-month-old baby girl, just didn't cut the starry-eyed image I had in mind as a writer in Paris. But combined with the one day a week Leroy started me with at *Chez Haynes*, I could pay the rent and begin to breathe, or at least not choke.

When I began that first one day a week as a dishwasher, I was over the moon—actually, I was over a large industrial tin sink with sludgy brown water dotted by bits of half-chewed lettuce floating on top. Finally, a job that put real coin in my hand and food in my belly. It was a job I could almost boast about, a job I could take to Orwell, look him in the eye, and not blink. Who was I to question how the norms of Leroy's business worked? He had an arrangement with the local police, so it followed we had an agreement with them too. Although, none of us mentioned it. Leroy looked after them, so they looked after him and his staff. And we looked after them. The age-old circle of life on the street. Over the years, the police checked on the restaurant several times. They would usually drop in early, just after 5 p.m. but well before we opened at 7 p.m. They would have to be blind not to see that we were all foreigners whose mastery of the Gallic language was pitiful at best. I would serve them a pastis or a glass of wine or a bottle of Heineken, depending on taste, while one of the waitresses hurried up the street to Leroy's place to let him know his friends were visiting. Sometimes the cops told us not to bother Leroy. They knew he might still be sleeping off a late night. We would chat for a few minutes, and they would leave. Never once did they ask for identification or question our right to work there. If Leroy hired us, it was okay by them.

Leroy employed young people as dishwashers, waitresses, and bartenders who were also writers, poets, photographers, painters, and dancers. He was generous and warm-hearted, one of those rare people who somehow hadn't managed to forget what it meant to be young. In Paris those were years without credit cards; copy machines were rare; even telephones were hard to come by. *Chez Haynes* was a safe haven. And our dreams of Paris would surely come true.

It is hard to think of the restaurant as gone. Like you, I have been up there, to 3 Rue Clauzel, a couple of times since it closed. Everything gone. Log façade, doors, curtains, Kon-Tiki hut. The world has moved on.

I often thought that he had that hut and those fake palms over the bar to remind him of his time soldiering in the Pacific at Guadalcanal.

There are lots of photos somewhere. What I would give to get the pictures that hung on his wall—the famous musicians and celebrities and, a few pictures of us workers that Leroy let us hang on the back wall among some of the greats. I particularly remember a Halloween photo of us all in North American style 'trick or treat' costumes. Not very *haute couture*. But matchless in an eccentric way. It was indicative of Leroy's sense of generosity and amusement that he let us put up some of our photos on the *Chez Haynes* walls.

I don't think anything could ever erase the first day I worked there. Leroy told me to transfer 20 kilos of raw chitlins from a large metal vat in the walk-in fridge to several smaller containers in the smaller fridges by the stoves. What the hell was this stuff? I'd never seen anything like it. Some kind of pig innards cloaked in congealed fat. It didn't give the impression of food. The smell was tactile. And not in a good way. It clung to the nostrils-- even the full diaper I had emptied earlier that afternoon smelled better. People actually ate this? Fried chicken gizzards I could understand—they were delicious—but this atrocity sliding through my fingers? Who did Leroy hate that much that he would feed it to them? On the other hand, if Louis Armstrong, Memphis Slim and James Baldwin could eat it, so could I. And I did. Not a whole lot of times. Never fully acquired the taste. But I did acquire an appreciation for everything else 'soul' he had on the menu. The gizzards were even better than chicken livers, which changed my whole outlook on liver. The gumbo was incredible. The black beans and dirty rice enriched the already perfect fried chicken and barbecue ribs. For a boy raised on Canadian prairie food, and for whom horseradish and black pepper were the height of exotic, this was an in-at-the-deep-end class in flavor. Not to mention that those staff dinners, just before opening, saved my life.

The food was always good, we had a choice from the entire menu, and that meal kept me in shape, and thin. Most days I had a snack at lunch. I knew I had a hot meal waiting for me in the evening.

I remember Leroy coming out of the kitchen one night, taking a moment and looking at us all sitting around the dinner table, eating his food and laughing about something ridiculous. He just shook his head. Then he said, 'when I opened this restaurant, I fed black musicians, now I'm feeding a bunch of white writers, artists and dancers.' He turned, shaking his head, muttering 'uhh-uhhh' and walked back into the kitchen. At that time, he was almost the same age as we are now. He had seen and done most of what there was to see and do. I could see he was wondering what this change in his staff amounted to. White kids were clearly not what he had anticipated. But he was also okay with it. Even paternal. Often grudgingly so. His eyes said it. We may not have been his first choice but, hell, we were what the deck had dealt him, and he went with it.

We're two old geezers now, Greg, over seventy, we thought we'd never reach this age. We're going to talk a little, and I don't care if this ever gets published.

Published? Are you kidding me? The word hardly has any meaning anymore. Back then selling a hundred copies of a book of my poems (twenty of which Leroy bought) was a major accomplishment, now anyone with an idea and a sentiment can 'publish' their 'work' to thousands in seconds. And that's the way it should be. For me, just being alive and breathing—'publishing my breath'—is accomplishment enough.

At least our kids and friends will appreciate it.

That would be nice.

They'll enjoy a good laugh.

2.

The Norse Goddess

I HAD GONE TO *CHEZ Haynes* to find out about that possible job. At 3 Rue Clauzel, I pushed open the saloon doors. A beautiful, blond woman strode out from behind the bar.

"How can I help you? We aren't open yet."

I asked about the job opening. She said she was the manageress. She told me her name was Astrid. And yes, she strode. She strode everywhere. That was how she moved through her life. Now she came up to me and said:

"Yes, we're looking for a bartender. Come by the lamp here on the bar, open your mouth."

She grabbed my chin in one hand, and a spoon in the other, and rattled it around my mouth. Clickety-clack, my molars took a beating.

"Good breath, good teeth, good bite, I was a dental assistant once," she explained, "I know about these things, anyway, you're hired. Have you ever tended bar?"

"No," I said, "but I'm a fast learner."

"It doesn't matter. I like you, she said. You start on Monday. Get yourself a book on mixology."

"Mixology?" I asked.

"Yeah, that's a fancy word for mixing cocktails which is another fancy word for making drinks to screw with people's heads. If you've never heard of the cocktail a client wants, then ask me or make it up. You're a good-looking kid, you know that? See you Monday at five in the afternoon. You prepare the bar, wash the glasses, get the wine and the hard stuff from the *cave*–that's the basement in French. We feed you, the restaurant opens at seven; we close at two in the morning."

And when I told her I didn't know much about oenology she said:

"Don't worry honey, a simple rule, I don't care what people tell you, the more the wine costs, the better it is."

The manageress was not there when I first visited the restaurant. Which would have been unusual because *Chez Haynes* was an obsession with her. Or was that with you? She did appear to like you. Whatever. There was no beautiful woman behind the bar when I stepped through that door for the first time. You were behind the bar. I can still recall the dusty red velvet curtain I had to push through after entering through the log-veneered saloon doors. I am sure the curtains were put there to keep out the draughts, but clearly not the riffraff. Let's face it, I was close to riffraff.

I want to say a few words about the saloon doors and curtains. The floor behind the bar was slightly elevated so I had a good view as soon as the curtains parted and before the saloon doors swung inward. Above and under the saloon doors I saw the clients' heads and feet before their bodies. I learned to size up people quickly. A white Russian sable hat? Ferragamo shoes? I knew what to expect from people wearing stuff worth thousands of dollars; I would nod to the waitresses and quietly say, 'check this out'.

There were no sable hats when I pushed through the curtains. There was the Kon-Tiki hut over the bar. And behind that bar, you, this brooding artist-type guy who said little, but over the next few hours let me know he was a painter and not a full-time bartender. I remember you said it with confidence. All these years later, I picture you in a dark turtleneck, but it could have been a white T-shirt. I ordered a beer; you gave me a Heineken in a Stella Artois glass and eventually, we started talking about art and philosophy—which is what I came to Paris for and what you were apparently doing. It was a tremendous argumentative dialogue which

I recall taking us through the night. It was also punctuated with Leroy coming out and telling you he didn't pay you to talk to poor white writers (or something like that) and telling me he hoped I wasn't looking for a free beer and then telling you to give me one anyway. I think he said 'or whatever he wants' — you gave me two or three. Or did some of that about Leroy come later? Lots came later. A month later, Leroy hired me; one night a week to start. Anyway, that's how I met you, and that's how I first came to *Chez Haynes*. No manageress. No mixology. No dental check-up.

But, hell, you know how the manageress was; you worked in the kitchen.

My memory of Astrid was she was all about business. She never sat down with us to eat. Not because she thought she was above us but because she was always moving. Yes, striding. Couldn't stop. When we asked her to join us or to take a load off and enjoy the evening meal, she would retort 'some people live to eat, but I eat to live'. When it came to food, function trumped form. And this in Paris of all places!

But Greg, you washed dishes, you made the salads, and Don was right there, he was the cook, remember? Don loved Astrid.

Oh, yes, I do remember that. Astrid, Don and you. A lively entertainment.

Don had lived with the manageress at one time. And one Saturday after work, Astrid, asked me out, and we went to a bistro nearby. We drank a few glasses, and she said we should skip supper and spend the night together. I told her I didn't think it was a good idea, but I did find her attractive. I was touched by what she said to me later that evening, after even more drinks. She said, 'you can just paint, I'll let you paint, and I'll make the money, I'll take care of you, of everything'. It was soft and moving. I didn't say anything, and in the following days and weeks, she never brought it up again. But when I went down to the cave in the evenings to get the wine for the night, she would flounce down the stairs, laughing and lifting her skirt, knickers ahoy, and she'd say, 'here, it's all yours, take it away'. And Don must have noticed she was flirting with me. He'd stand by the kitchen door and watch the steps going down to the *cave,* and he held a carving knife behind his back. You told me all that.

You had a right to know.

Scared the daylights out of me, every time I went down there for the wine, she'd come hopping down, and I imagined Don with that knife. I always wondered how she handled him. She must have told him something, after all.

Probably not. But he wasn't blind. Even though they were no longer a formal couple, he still loved the woman. On occasion, he would leave the kitchen—apron stained with blood from cutting up chicken and spareribs all evening—walk past me to the end of the hallway and survey the dining room. If I suggested he was watching you when you and Astrid descended into the cave, that was probably true. And if I said he did often have his knife in hand, sometimes behind his back, that was also true. So, the path to your demise, bleeding out behind the bar, was certainly there. Although when I told you of his macabre intentions, I may have been embellishing them to suggest more interesting dramatic possibilities than the evidence would support. The fact is you survived intact.

Some evenings when there was a lull in the dinner conversation, you'd say, I wonder if one of us will be dead by this time next year. That freaked out most of the staff, except for Leroy, who would let out a loud guffaw.

I think I said something like 'statistics suggest that this time next year one of us around this table will be dead. And since you are the oldest, Rafael, it will probably be you'. At the table, you went ghostly white. Neither of us mentioned Don, although I think some of the waitresses knew.

And let's face it, the waitresses were all beauties, and Leroy knew many clients came into his joint to gawk and stayed to dine and got plastered trying to chat up the girls.

However eccentric Leroy was in his own life, he stayed true to gender roles in the restaurant; men behind the bar, in the kitchen and over the sink, and women were servers and managers. It felt somewhat odd in Paris where waiters were predominantly men.

Astrid had a strange way with the clients, too, especially those who tried to show off. When one asked about the *chili con carne*, whether it was spicy and hot, she would say, 'Hot? Are you fucking kidding me? It'll pop your hemorrhoids like there's no tomorrow and make the ladies' nipples stand up like machine gun barrels, take my word for it', and she'd dare the men to say otherwise, as she stood there in her volcano-shaped fifties bra. And man, did the clients come back asking for more? They loved her.

She certainly was a feature. And I grant you she was attractive, but possibly not stunning. You must remember, (how do I put this delicately), you are five years older than me, Rafael. And she was a good eight years older than you. So, to me, she was old. Or oldish. Good-looking oldish. Norse-goddess-beautiful. Tall, long blond hair, usually piled up on her head, statuesque and with large breasts accentuated, as you say, by whatever she was wearing under her sweater. The closest I ever got to your experience was preparing salads in the narrow hallway between the kitchen and the dining room. She would go into the kitchen to say something to Don, return along the hallway, turn sideways to squeeze by me, pause, shove her breasts into my back, rub them back and forth and then fly off to attend to a customer. I cannot say it was disagreeable. Not like Helen, the exceptionally large Welsh waitress, whom Don called the 'fullback', and who was unable to pass by me without her body shoving me face-first into the espresso machine. When I saw her coming, two or three plates delicately balanced, I would have to duck into the toilet to let her by.

Those first days I was on the *qui vive*, I wasn't going to screw up this job. Stay alert, see how things flow, learn the unspoken rules and rituals. This job allows me to paint during the day. 'Don't forget that' I told myself over and over again.

You always had your eye on the goal. 'Focus' and 'organization' were your mantras. There was a reason we were all there. And Norse goddess or not, you took it seriously.

3.

The Cook and the Goldfish

DON, THE COOK, WAS A rather strange and inscrutable man. I never knew much about him except that he pined for the blond manageress. He had come to Paris with Leroy from Berlin. His mother was Sicilian, his father a black GI. I never knew where Don had grown up; he knew no Italian but spoke French well, better than Leroy. He wasn't educated, as was Leroy, who had received an MA from Morehouse College in Atlanta, Georgia.

In my first year at *Chez Haynes*, I spent a lot of time with Don. As the resident dishwasher, the small kitchen, the narrow salad and coffee-making hallway and the tiny toilet were the limits of my working life. And Don was my companion of sorts. I hesitate to say I was Sancho Panza to his Don Quixote, but in the kitchen, knife in hand, constantly glancing over the top of his glasses, wiping his hands on his apron, slinging one pan after another from burner to burner, calling out the orders, he was a man on a quest, unflinching and relentless. I on the other hand blundered around under his commands, often mistaking chicken gizzards for chicken livers and under the illusion that a barely visible drop of rib sauce on an otherwise almost washed plate was perfectly fine. Don was just going to slap another order of ribs on it anyway. Now I know why he was constantly looking over his glasses—checking my work. He had seen it all and knew how easy it was to get it right. If he could get the ribs perfect, how hard was it for me, my arms deep into a soapy, suds-filled metal sink to take a moment and scrub a little harder? Fortunately, his bark, while loud, was essentially toothless. And he could be very funny. Nothing phased him. I am sure he preferred *Chez Haynes* during the musician days over our writer-artist-dancer-actor antics, but he was respectful, and if we were happy working for 90F to his 500F a night, that was our business.

Don did the cooking under Leroy's supervision. Don was basically a racist, which may sound odd, but it's the truth. Leroy paid him damn good money. Don had no overhead, no children to support, and from what we learned later he lived simply. He had some goldfish, Astrid told me. He liked jazz, and when the drummer Kenny Clarke or the pianist Memphis Slim came around, Don would come out from the kitchen and chat with them. Don, like Leroy, played the horses and, unlike Leroy, prided himself on never reading a book. Now in retrospect, I realize it must have been emotionally hard, even painful psychologically, for Don to watch his blond Astrid being courted by the high and mighty. The swaggering businessmen, and bohemian sleaze-balls, who slipped her their calling cards or scribbled addresses and phone numbers on a napkin.

I don't remember much detailed supervision by Leroy. He did set the menu and was exceedingly particular about the food being presented the right way and tasting as it should. But his quality control was intermittent and random, sometimes, affected by more than a few glasses of whisky. He knew he needed Don to make that kitchen work. And he trusted him even if they were different as right and wrong, each of them taking hold of both sides of that stick at some point or other. Don's racism was a bizarre feature of the man, stark against the background of Leroy's essential humanity. It was noteworthy that he would engage us in that debate—I'm not sure he bought it all. Certainly, he spouted an appreciation for the order and purity of the Nazis and claimed their racist views were acceptable collateral damage. I was never sure if he was just goading our wide-eyed youth. I never witnessed he and Leroy take on the subject in an argument. Maybe they had learned to stay clear of each other on that account.

I never had any long talks with Don. He sensed I didn't care too much about food. Yet I remember clearly one evening when he talked about making a good omelet. He said timing was everything in the restaurant business. You beat the eggs, heat up the butter in the frying pan, then pour in the eggs on the sizzling butter and then, and this was important, wait a few seconds before lifting the frying pan about thirty centimeters above the flame for a few seconds and then lowering it back on the flame and pushing the omelet edges a little toward the center. You do this a few times depending on how runny you want your omelet, or as the French say, *baveuse*, which means drooling or drooly if such a word exists in English. It takes time Don said, and in the restaurant, he didn't have time to make every omelet so elaborately. I tried his method later and it was true, done slowly like Don said, you got a perfect omelet.

He was a perfectionist. Not only in food preparation. But also, in appearance. Everything was in place. It was hard not to understand his obsession with the 'blond goddess' in terms of this perfectionist and racist, landscape. And the pain it eventually brought him. My most vivid memory of him was at one of the after-work parties we organized—someone's leaving party or a birthday bash—but it was late, three or four in the morning. We were all high and Don was singing along to the song *By the Time I Get to Phoenix*. It was the Isaac Hayes version, almost 20 minutes long with an introduction about a man's love for an unfaithful woman who cheated on him, year after year, but he would always give her another chance. Until finally he couldn't take it anymore and, early in the morning, he leaves her. Then the song begins. His eyes closed, Don lay back into the chair, slowly shaking his head back and forth with the music—we all knew of whom he was thinking. At first, he was singing along, but then near the end, he added his own lyrics: "cold bitch; cold bitch," he whispered softly under his breath; "cold bitch" over and over, even after the song ended. It was powerful stuff. We were all moved by his pain.

In the nineties, I went to see Don when he was dying in a hospital near the Gare du Nord. He didn't recognize me. I was there with Quincy, one of the waitresses who had also known him in the Pigalle days. Don was buried in the cemetery of Pantin, east of Paris, the biggest in Europe. There were four other people there, all of us waiting for the gravedigger to dig the hole for the unmarked pine coffin. The man had spray-painted four white lines, roughly the size of the pine coffin, on the grass. He dug out the oblong square hole in front of us. He was in a full sweat by the time he finished. He and his assistant lifted up the coffin and plunked it into the hole. They shoveled the earth back on top. I clearly remember the pitter-patter noise of the earth as it hit the coffin. Then with their shovels, the two men patted down the mound of earth. 'With time' the gravedigger said, 'it'll flatten down'. Into the grass, he hammered a wooden stake with a sign with Don's name. There were no relatives present, only the musicians and fellow *turfistes*, horse racing buddies. There was in me a feeling of leaden solitude, not for me but for Don. Somehow, it seemed to me at that moment that so many Americans never put down roots of any kind in the French capital; they live on an island with other lonely Americans. The only phrase I could come up with was *so far from home*. Where had Don played as a child, learned to ride a bicycle, first danced with a girl? Had he loved anyone except for his blond goddess in Pigalle? She wasn't at the funeral.

I confess when you informed me of Don's death, it was different than when I learned of Leroy's death in 1984. Leroy was the same age as my father and there were associations between the two in my feelings. Don was different somehow. He kept to himself. I suspect what you describe of the funeral was how he may have wanted it. I hope so. As for putting down roots in the French capital, Leroy and Don shared that. But I am not sure how deep those roots went. They undeniably stretched to the day-to-day people and activities in the city, but at no time did I observe a profound depth of feeling for the city. In Leroy's case, there was no suggestion he missed his original American roots, as much as he may have wanted to escape them. He was saddened by them but often energized by them. It took very little to evoke a story from his time growing up in the South. And Chicago in the twenties and thirties: great stories, full of humor and pathos and dark memories. And, of course, the restaurant continually brought America to his door. The Americans, black and white—mainly black—came to pay homage, with their stories and music and admiration. It was a rich tapestry. On the other hand, I do not remember anyone coming to the restaurant for Don. The details of Don's life, Don's roots, Don's origins, remain a mystery to me.

It took me a good half hour to walk out of the Pantin cemetery, and at the Porte de la Villette, I walked under the *boulevard périphérique* and decided to keep on walking. I circled Place de Stalingrad, headed down Quai de Jemmapes, then along the Canal Saint Martin to the Bastille. There were a few fishermen sitting by the water. I found it surreal that after Saint Martin the canal disappeared underground where it was lit by daylight coming in through large, circular openings covered by a grill in the walkway above. Did the men manning underground barges feed the fish in the dark water beneath? I thought of Don's goldfish. Who had them now? Those fish are known for their extremely short memories. I walked all the way to my apartment near the Bastille. In the *Chez Haynes* days, I lived near the Centre Pompidou, which in those days was just a gigantic hole in the ground, an urban grave.

Don's goldfish would have made a classic permanent exhibition in the Pompidou Centre.

I agree, but Don wouldn't have given a whit about the museum. The guards would have to feed those babies once in a while. And when the fish croaked? What then?

Okay, maybe not a permanent exhibition. But classic, nevertheless.

As I took out my apartment key, my *carte orange* fluttered to the floor.

Like the fish? Orange and eventually lifeless?

4.

Cleaning for San Fernando

At *Chez Haynes*, it was warm in the winter, and we were fed; these were two buffers against hardship. And if I indulged in feeling sorry for myself, Alicia, the Spanish cleaning lady at the restaurant, always lifted my spirits. She and I crossed paths every evening; she was finishing her cleaning as I arrived. As I set up the bar and washed glasses, we chatted in Spanish. She was from Sevilla and was married, and her husband worked the night shift for the French railroads, the SNCF, *Société National de Chemins de Fer.* They had come to France as a newly married couple, to get away from Franco, and now they were in their forties. Some evenings, just like that, Alicia or I would say 'that Bastard Franco finally died'. He had died in November 1975.

That Bastard's *Guardia Civil* beat me up on one of the less savory streets of Barcelona in late 1971. That scared the living daylights out of me.

Alicia called him *el cabrón de Paco Franco*, the Billy goat Paco Franco.

Much too kind an epithet. I assume it conveyed a more scathing humiliation of the old dictator in the Spain of the time. It does not capture my memory of Alicia. Quiet and understated. If you had not mentioned her, I am not sure she would have come easily, or at all, to my mind.

During the day, before she came into the restaurant, Alicia cleaned fancy apartments in the sixteenth *arrondissement* in Paris. She looked worn out, her face was prematurely lined from years of exhausting work, but when she spoke Spanish, her face lit up. She was always in a good mood. One evening she told me she and her husband were planning a visit to Sevilla to see her relatives, but the real purpose of the trip, she confided, was to buy a plot for herself and her husband in the San Fernando Cemetery. How about an apartment first, I asked her. First, we serve God, she said. She loved bullfights, and she had only been to the Fair of Sevilla once in her teens. Rarely did she mention her daughter, who was her cross to bear. Why? 'She sleeps around, Alicia' said, 'and seems to have a lot of money all the time'.

I want to say Alicia was an inspiration, but I do not think I would have said that then. Nor now. I remember she worked incredibly hard and did not complain. At least not to us. I could not speak to her in Spanish, and I think her French was about the same as mine so our conversations were full of head nods and smiles, the kind that said we would both appreciate getting to know each other a little more if the curse of Babel permitted. But it didn't. I do remember her referring to her teenage daughter on more than one occasion. Even in our threadlike exchanges, I could see it was a troubling preoccupation, and that her smiles and nods could only suggest there was a deeper story there.

I mention Alicia because she was a reminder not to complain or feel sorry for myself. And if she was ever depressed Alicia never once let it show. To this day I think of her often and I hope she and her husband did buy an apartment in Sevilla and retired there. But by now they're probably with San Fernando.

Realizing the eternal peace of her first investment? My overwhelming sense of Alicia as I think back now is how cheerful she was. Never a mean word or nasty gesture. Always smiles. And you are right, she was a reminder of how fortunate we were back then. Despite our lack of money, we chose it. But we had support systems, not the least of which were our education and privilege. We could pursue idiocy and call it experimentation. While we aspired to whatever nonsensical ideas of artistic immortality prevailed back then, Alicia aspired to a cemetery plot. I could have learned a lot more about things that matter if I had been wise enough to stop a while and listen more carefully. But wisdom was not abundant back then.

At Christmas, Leroy gave her two thousand francs as a bonus. That was a lot of money in those days, about 400 dollars.

That was pure Leroy.

The lack of money sometimes triggered depressions and feelings of failure in me. But it was seldom debilitating. At the restaurant, we rarely talked about our feelings. The work at *Chez Haynes* kept me busy, there was little time to mope and whine. I talked about my painting. You spoke of your poetry and your plays. We didn't realize it then, but *Chez Haynes* was an antechamber of sorts or a safe zone where we worked on the first moves to pursue our dreams. A few years later, I understood this when there were no more safe zones, and depression became a recurring beast in my psyche.

And San Fernando beckoned.

5.

La carte orange and *les toilettes à la turque*

My *carte orange* landed silently on the landing parquet by my apartment door and at the moment my memory came alive. I remembered how every first of the month you'd burst into the restaurant, Greg, holding your *carte orange* in the air, then announce, 'here it is, ladies and gents, got my carte orange for the month, I›m set, I can go anywhere in Paris with this piece of plastic; that's like going anywhere in the world, as we all know right now Paris is the world.' The *carte orange* was a subway pass with your picture on it. You renewed it once a month, and it allowed you to travel wherever and as often as you wanted on the metro and buses of Paris. The pass was second class, unless you splurged. In those days the metro had first class carriages too.

Thank you for mentioning *la carte orange*. I will confess to going a bit overboard with its praise—maybe more than a bit overboard. The day, once a month, when I purchased that small new paper *billet* for my *carte orange* was sublime. I almost said 'somewhat sublime' but it really was sublime. Mobility was freedom. It awarded me freedom. To Paris no less. I still recall one very specific day when I purchased a monthly ticket in one of the metro stations on *ligne 2*—from the *Porte d'Orléans* to the *Porte de*

Clignancourt line. My line. I remember it because I also picked up a brand-new plastic cover the card slipped into. Laura was with me. I remember holding up the card in its clean new plastic sleeve and saying to her with all sincerity that this single purchase gave me more pleasure than any other thing I bought in Paris. Admittedly, I was not buying a lot of stuff back then, but it pleased me more than buying beer, wine, food—not trivial purchases. I'm sure she thought I was crazy. She laughed. I think with me. Not at me. Maybe a bit of both.

You must remember, in the first three years of my stay in Paris—until eventually securing a *carte de séjour* on the basis of being a "poet" (the benefits of which never came close to those offered by a *carte orange*)—I was an undocumented immigrant, or whatever the relevant authorities may have called it back then. I will give them their due; they never cared about my presence much, no matter how dreadfully I disfigured their language. I found their disinterest in me, always with an underlying air of disdain, positively liberating. Despite being scowled at and frowned on for our all too frequent frivolous and inane public displays of lunacy—'American Infantilism' according to the disapproving French wife of one of our friends—we were grudgingly tolerated.

When I look back on it now, I understand my whiteness cloaked in a student-artist façade provided me with a dispensation not everyone was afforded. The idea that I might be deported never entered my mind. After all, I had my *carte orange*. My photo and name were on it. It gave me a Parisian identity of sorts. More importantly it gave unlimited travel throughout Paris and its banlieue. All for 40 francs––eight dollars. It was affordable. I could earn that in four hours at *Chez Haynes*. It was like giving a pass to Disneyland to a seven-year-old today, except this pass was to a land much larger, much more exciting, much more alive—an historic and cultural utopia.

On winter days, the metro was also a respite from the cold. *Chez Haynes* was a warm place too, but in general, keeping your apartment warm, no matter how small, in the Paris winters was a problem. Few people have written about the indoor heating issue in Paris; we often hung out in cafés and bistros. We dreaded the electricity bill, and we thought twice about ramping up the electric heaters. We found ingenious ways of slowing down the electricity meter by placing a hefty magnet on top of it or with a jeweler's drill making a minute hole and slipping in a piano wire to block the spinning cogwheel. We spattered paint on the meter to camouflage the hole for the piano wire, and of course, we made sure to take out the wire or the magnet when the meter reader came around.

We did what we had to do to live. That and a bit of luck sufficed. And we did have luck. Finding my flat was a genuine fluke—a friend of a friend of a friend thing. Harry and his cousin Wendy came to my rescue again. I never worked with Wendy at *Chez Haynes*, but I remember an odd story which Harry told about her riding on the subway with her mother who was visiting her from Pennsylvania. They were sitting on the *strapontins*, the fold-down seats next to the doors. At one of the metro stations the door opened and a strange man on the platform suddenly reached through the door and grabbed Wendy's breasts. Just for a moment. Then the door shut, and the metro continued on. After a moment's silence, Wendy's mother said: 'You know Wendy, I think that young man thought he knew you', assuming, perhaps, Wendy had a multitude of romantic liaisons stretched across the Paris Metro system.

I worked briefly with Wendy at Haynes. I never got to know her. She sounds like a person willing to take risks, open to adventure. Having her breasts fondled, albeit briefly in public and not going ape shit about it, well, that makes for a cool head. In those days in Paris going to the cops with this story about male aggressive behavior wouldn't have done much good. That, I'm sure of.

Wendy's friend was a forty-year-old American woman who was unexpectedly leaving for Cairo with her brand-new Egyptian boyfriend. She was going all in on him and needed to sublet her flat near Place d'Alésia in the 14th *arrondissement* quickly. She guaranteed me three months which even I thought was optimistic. But the bet must have paid off because she never returned, and I was able to convert the flat into my name six months later. Only a month into my stay, with no papers—not even a *carte orange*—and I had a permanent home.

Not that my living space was luxurious, or even blue-collar. It consisted of two maid's rooms on the top floor of a five-floor walk-up building. The building was nice in a bourgeois sort of way, with thick carpet on the stairway until the last set of stairs. The maids, I guess, did not deserve carpet. There were five rooms in total on the top floor. Except for my two rooms, they were all empty. Nobody ever came up to the top floor but me. My two rooms were in the middle, linked by a doorway, knocked through to make it look like it was an apartment. The two doors to the corridor remained, one of which was permanently locked and the other functioned as my front door. It entered what became my living room. The finished look didn't include much of a kitchen—a short counter with a little sink, cordoned off with a couple of ceiling high cupboards dividing it from my bedroom. So, all in all, not bad. Except there was no bathroom. There was a shared 'Turkish toilet' (hole in the floor) down the hall, and a foldout shower hanging off the inside of the front door in my living room. On the other hand, both rooms had large beautiful French windows which opened out onto a medium size cobblestone square. The view 'out' was incomparable, even if the view 'in' had much to be desired.

It was impossible to get in or out of the apartment if the shower was not folded up. So, each time I took a shower, I had to unfold the plastic platform from the front door, pull a shower curtain around the platform, hook up a shower hose to the tap in the small hot water heater over the kitchen sink, connect another hose from a pump underneath the shower platform to siphon the used water back into the sink, get in and turn on the water. *Voilà!* Afterwards I folded the whole unit back up and pushed it back against the door. It worked well when I remembered to turn on the pump. Which I mostly did. But not always. As for the WC, I was the only one living on the top floor, so it was all mine. Along with porcelain footpads next to the porcelain hole in floor, the room had a sink and a mirror and a soap dispenser. I disinfected them all, thoroughly cleaned the room and painted it. I would be genuinely hard put to say I have had a better, more hygienic toilet since then.

Mais oui, mon ami. À la turque. We also called them squat jobs. And when you flushed and weren't out of there fast enough you got a urine shine on your shoes. And don't forget the toilet paper or your apartment key. Down the hall you could find yourself, without paper, without your apartment key and your pants down by your ankles.

You are right! It was all mine, so I sometimes walked naked down the corridor in the early morning. Until the day my apartment door closed (the wind?) and locked behind me. I had no key with me and hesitated to call for assistance as I was in a state of complete undress. The doors were solid, but I leaned back against the stairwell banister and eventually kicked the unused door open. I was also able to repair the lock, but there was a permanent crack in the door which I disguised with paint. Thereafter, I hid a second key in *la turque* under the sink.

There were squat jobs in most bistros, but if you got the urge and rushed into a café you'd see a neat little sign, oh so beautifully lettered, on the zinc counter: *l'utilisation des toilettes est reservée aux consommateurs*. You can only use the toilettes if you buy something. Most often you were in a rush, and you quickly ordered a coffee, paid, and headed down the steep stairs to the WC. Or if you only had to pee you could use those disgusting *vespassennes*, circular, metal structures on the sidewalks--only for men. You'd walk into these things and urinate. People walking by could see your legs beneath the metal enclosure and hear the pee as it spattered against the metal. How come you never read about that in the guidebooks? I must say, the French were very sanguine when it came to poop and pee. Nothing to be ashamed of, bodily functions. They didn't have many indoor toilets, and they used a lot of perfume to keep the smell camouflaged and the perfume industry thriving. Although some days riding in the metro was an olfactory experience hard to ignore.

If my WC was your basic, rudimentary Parisian commode circa 1970, my reward was a telephone—a semi miracle. The waiting list to get a telephone back then was six years. I also had radiator heat included in my rent. It worked brilliantly for three seasons, disappearing in the winter. So free heat when my neighbors with the large apartments below were not using it—which they tended to do when the air turned cold. My little electric heater became an important and faithful companion until, you will remember, it disappeared into the bathroom of your second studio at 67 Rue de la Roquette when I left for London.

Back to the *carte orange*. It was for working stiffs basically, but it gave us a sense of freedom. We never took taxis; that was for tourists. Every franc counted, and the *carte orange* guaranteed our mobility.

And *la turque* guaranteed our wellbeing.

My *toilette à la turque* was still down the hall, and the hot water was iffy because some days, the Rube Goldberg contraption that heated the water refused to work. The gas came from a gas bottle underneath the sink, and that was iffy too, but my rent was cheap, and we knew we'd have one good meal a day at *Chez Haynes,* bless Leroy's heart. That man was a cultural benefactor of the highest order; he enabled many artists and writers and actors and dancers to pursue their dreams in Paris. If you had the crazy idea of applying for any help from the government, you had to get legal, and we soon learned that those artists who did get a cheap artist studio had connections in the ministry of culture, which usually meant they had a relative there or were sleeping with their connection.

Government help? For heat? For food? For clothing? Really? Until you mentioned it, it had never ever occurred to me. I was just happy not to spend time in their correctional institutions. Although, after a bout of tonsillitis, I did spend a free week in the hospital having my heart examined every which way but up. I remember there were lots and lots of medical students in and out of my room all the time. So, I paid for my stay by being an instructional prop. *Chez Haynes* was our social safety net. It provided a warm home, hot meals, and talk, lots and lots of talk. Throw in a *carte orange*, baguettes, and my own private *toilette à la turque* and life was good.

6.

Under the Mountain

Bread was something we could always afford. You would say you had your baguette, for a few days at least. A baguette a day kept me fed, a little constipated too, the staff of life. Maybe that's pushing it. A baguette in hand, I could walk into an *épicerie* and buy some slices of ham, or in the Latin Quarter I would stuff a sizzling merguez into half a baguette, and that was a good meal.

Yes. The good life was richly enhanced by the baguette. And its luxuries. Like butter. Oh, the butter. A fresh baguette with Parisian butter? That's a four-star meal in itself. Throw in the ham, the cheese, and the merguez? A self-indulgence that makes me salivate, even as I write 45 years later.

There was even a baguette painted blue in the Museum of Modern art, a piece of Dada art by Man Ray. Baguettes become as hard as wood, a baked baseball bat, it could be used as a weapon.

I like Man Ray even more now.

Bit of trivia for you. His real name was Emmanuel Radnitzky.

Fantastic name play. As in his work, too. Especially his film *Retour de Raison*, which was anything but. I think Leroy had a sketch or doodle of his on a napkin. Painting a hardened baguette blue may have been a step too far. A rigid baguette is still recoverable, no matter how hard. And, as *pain perdu*––French toast—it is almost as good. If it's breakfast, sometimes even better. It does deserve to be in a museum, whatever the color. Talking about sealing and painting everyday objects, are you going to mention the object we sealed and painted and sent out to announce your first one man show in Paris?

I'll get to that show later. Bakeries first. I'd go into a *boulangerie* to buy a baguette, and since I was always hungry, especially on Sundays around noon, buying only a baguette was hard.

Yes, maybe not such a good topic while talking about bread.

In French bakeries––my God, what a display––my eyes wandered over the sparkling glass shelves with all those pastries on show, so many shapes and sizes and flavors, the *Paris-Brests, the pains aux raisins, the croissants aux amandes,* and the *congolais.* Ah, those were the worst, a pure sugar high, the best thing to have when you got the munchies after smoking a joint. The *congolais* was a conic shaped, little mountain of ground coconut and a lot of sugar, and there were the *palmiers* too, *financiers*, and the *madeleines.*

And you told Don you were not much into food? Sounds like your eyes were well schooled.

Yes of course, I knew of Marcel Proust and his damn *madeleines.* When I ate one, I thought I was eating a pastry full of chopped letters. Good old Marcel, under the guise of literary literature, he was the greatest gossip of all time, *une sacrée commère, celui-là.*

On those few occasions, when finances permitted and gastronomic desires insisted, I drifted towards the savory items on the shelves. Sugar rarely called to me like a good *croque monsieur* or, even better, a *croque madame*. Essentially versions of a toasted cheese and ham sandwich. But what versions they were! Someday I will peruse Proust for references. Or Balzac or Sartre. Did they eat *croque monsieurs* and admit it? Surely, Camus must have.

The point I'm trying to make here is that you might go into a bakery for a baguette, and I'll add here that I liked mine *pas trop cuite*, that is to say underdone, like steak tartare, baguette tartare, because these were less crispy. I thought for some reason that if the *baguette* was under-cooked, I could taste the dough better, there was less burned stuff, and it was more nutritious; the burnt dough was useless and hard on the gums. To walk out of a Parisian bakery with only a baguette is hard to pull off, especially if you're hungry. You pay for the baguette, and as you're leaving, you turn around and say I'll take a *croissant aux amandes* too. Damn!

Somehow, an under-cooked baguette sounds sacrilegious (*sacré bleu!*) to me. I have no memory of having eaten one, or an over-cooked one for that matter. Not that I would have thrown it away. Not then. Not even now. And now I can afford to. I will grant you the point about *les croissants*. A wonderful, wonderful treat. Especially with a *café crème*. Although, back then, the cost-to-calorie ratio was a bit high to make them a regular part of my day-to-day existence. Baguettes, on the other hand, came very close to matching the pleasure of a *carte orange*. They, too, were affordable. And supported life. Even when they came after an almost Ionesco-like dialogue.

Not long after I moved into my two room *chambre de bonne* flat, I found a nearby boulangerie that served fabulous baguettes. It was the closest and the first one I went into. To me, all boulangeries in Paris served fabulous baguettes. Anyway, every morning, I went there for my baguette, usually stood in line for a few minutes, would then be summoned for my order: "*Monsieur?*" and the following exchange would happen. Day after day after day.

Server: *Monsieur?*

Me: *Une baguette s'il vous plaît.*

Server: *Deux?*

Me (speaking my syllables slowly) *Non, une seu-le-ment.*

Server (wide eyes) hands me a single baguette and I give her 2F10.

This must have happened a dozen times. Usually, the same server but occasionally a different one. Never a smile. Maybe it was too busy, or this was just Paris?

Paris was a tough city; it could be cold and mean and rude. You didn't get many breaks, that was why Leroy was such a rarity. We all have heard of the proverbial neighbor on your floor. You can live for years on the same floor and all you'll ever get, if you get it all, is a cold *bonjour* from the person across your landing. There are exceptions, of course, but not many.

This incident was more cool eccentricity than cold rudeness. The *boulangère* always asked me if I wanted two after I ordered one. And each time, for a moment, as they handed me the baguette, they looked at me as if I was borderline insane. It was a daily conundrum that baffled me for months. You finally solved the puzzle when you waited with me one day while I got my morning baguette. We went in and on cue, the exchange happened. I just shrugged at you—what's up with that? As we left, you told me the problem was my French pronunciation: my *une* was incomprehensible, and my *seulement* sounded like *sous-le-mont*, as in *under the mountain*. As if I was suggesting a romantic tryst on a quiet hillside. So, what transpired was:

Server: Sir?

Me: (something) baguette please

Server: two?

Me: No, (something) under the mountain

It was a wonder I was able to buy anything to eat at all. She probably thought it was a kind of American slang for sex.

The thing about *boulangeries* is that the women running the bakery, the b*oulangères*, were always good-looking, well-dressed in crispy clothes, and their aprons had traces of flour.

She was cute. There was a reason I kept going back.

The same thing was usually true with pharmacists and *coiffeuses*. I'd see them through the window, but I never went into a coiffure salon.

Attractive and intimidating was a lethal combination?

I cut my own hair with a comb-like instrument with a razor blade, and depending on how you set it, as you pulled this thing through your hair, it cut it at the desired length. I saved myself quite a lot of money. I never had anything dry-cleaned either; it was too expensive, and I did my own sewing also, buttons too and even zippers.

But not as lethal as being broke?

With that and what we saved on baguettes and the *carte orange*--what did we do? We bought books, usually second-hand books, at Shakespeare and Co. on the left bank, across from Notre Dame. Sometimes we bought new books at WHSmith on Rivoli, or at Brentano's near the Opera. How to explain this? Baguette and *carte orange* dovetailed into reading and literature. Books were what we cared about.

Bread and books. Two more essentials. Shakespeare and Co. will always be dear to my heart. The first real bookstore to sell my book of poetry. And to host a reading I gave there. George Whitman, the founder, was a dedicated and friendly guy. I remember him as being serious about what he was doing. Creating a place for writers and artists to hang out and do what they do. Along with the big literary names who passed through—Allen Ginsberg, William Burroughs, Anaïs Nin, William Styron, Henry Miller, Lawrence Durrell, James Baldwin—hundreds of young writers made the pilgrimage as well. George was remarkably open to selling small press editions of their poetry and other writing. Such as ours. One Christmas I gave every one of our *Chez Haynes* company of friends and artists books which I bought there. It made Christmas shopping easy that year. A dozen or so volumes of poetry by young, lesser-known poets who lived under the mountain of celebrated names, and who had graced Shakespeare and Co. over the previous two and a half decades since its opening in 1951. Most of the books were covered with dust and curled up at the corners—each one different, and each one with a story of poems to share.

7.

Genghis

THE FIRST NIGHT WORKING AT the bar, the manageress helped me a little. After that first night I was on my own. I cleaned the glasses from the previous night, and by cleaning, I mean not only washing but also drying each glass with a dishtowel. I had brought up the wine and hard liquor from the basement. Then we ate supper, waitresses, the dishwasher, and salad maker. I looked forward to the communal dinners, it was a moment of banter and relaxation, and you were always coming up with jokes and puns that had us roaring with laughter. By seven, we were at our posts, the waitresses in front of the bar and I behind it. You were in the kitchen with your hands deep in the dishwater. I know you hated it.

I can't say I hated it. Some of it, of course, was unpleasant. Who likes standing over a deep sink, sweat pouring down their face? It was an assembly line which consisted of just me, one dish after another slopping through the process: scrape, dunk, scrub, rinse. I was a machine. On the other hand, the dishes did air dry, so I did not suffer the torment of wiping down a wine glass or two. More importantly, it paid the bills. Money was scarce. You may not remember but up until the time Leroy hired me, my main source of income was as a live-out au pair, taking care of four-month-old Clemence for six hours a day, three days a week. Wonderful little girl with terrific parents but even with her nap times, it did not leave much time for writing. I vastly improved my diaper skills, and my babbling, both of which came in handy later with my three boys. Dishwashing, on the other hand, afforded me Orwellian aspirations and vaguely adult conversation around the dinner table.

The salad making part of my duties provided some relief. It gave me a little escape time from the fiery heat of the kitchen, down the narrow hall into a kind of purgatory, from where I could just see and hear the bubbling commotion and enjoyment in the dining areas. That is also where Leroy would sit when he was in. He enjoyed preparing the different salad fixings, but, even more, I think he enjoyed eavesdropping on the clientele and watching them engage with the soul food ambiance he had created for them in his restaurant. First and foremost, he was theatrical: in his film work, in his stories, and in his restaurant. Once he had prepared all the ingredients, the salads were easy for me to throw together, and we would often talk. Depending on his mood or the depth of his hangover.

Hangovers. Years later my hangovers were what I dreaded. I loved the buzz and the loosening up of my brain when I drank; and even as I was having a good time, I told myself this time it'll be different, I won't have a hangover like a truck. Or, I am drinking single malt whisky tonight, good scotch doesn't give you a hangover. And so on.

You were young. Your bad nights were not as bad as his. Not then. On bad nights he was morose and quiet, sometimes mean but never hurtful. On good nights he was great. It was on one of those nights he told me my favorite Leroy story. It happened when he was living in Chicago: during Prohibition. I think he said he was about 12 or 13 years old. Leroy was born in 1914 so that would place the incident sometime in the mid-nineteen twenties. Al Capone days. Back then, he helped his father who had a job cleaning a speakeasy in the morning. They would drive into the city, some distance from wherever they were living, in an old third or fourth-hand car—'a jalopy, mostly made of rust', is how I remember him describing it. His father called it 'Jesus', hoping I assume that a little spiritual help would keep the pieces of the car together another day. One morning the rust didn't quite hold together. The car broke down, still miles from its destination. It took hours to repair it sufficiently to sputter the rest of the way in, hoping they still had a job. When they arrived, the speakeasy door had been blown off its hinges by an explosive attached to the lock, ignited by the key. Its force killed the assistant manager who opened the speakeasy that morning. Normally, Leroy and his father would have been first there to open up and start the cleaning. But on this day the breakdown of their car had spared their lives. At this point in the story, Leroy smiled broadly, his eyes twinkling, his actor's voice resonating in a spiritual tone, and he said: "so nobody can tell me Jesus don't save. I know he does. He saved my black ass!" and he would roll back on his chair in laughter, as did I and a couple of the waitresses who had stopped to listen.

What a great story! A car called Jesus.

And I am sure it is mostly true. I wish I could do the tale justice. He was a natural storyteller. Dishwashing and salads beat making cocktails on those nights. Although making cocktails could be fun.

You want to know about the cocktails?

Remind me.

I have forgotten many of them. I do recall making Sidecars, Whisky Sours, Brandy Alexanders, Manhattans, Tequila Sunrises, Blue Lagoons, classical Martinis, Gin Fizzes, and there was the artichoke liqueur Fernet Branca, vile stuff, but good for hangovers, and the poetically named *feuille morte*, made of pastis and grenadine, never liked it myself, and the *kirs*, champagne with *crème de cassis* was called *kir royal*, with white wine simply *kir*, and with red wine *un carabinier*. There were more brews and mixtures; some were stirred, others shaken, and garnished with Angostura bitters, olives, onions, cherries. Whenever somebody ordered a pure tequila with the lemon and side dish of salt, I would first point out the worm in the bottle before serving the drink, just to make sure the clients knew what they were drinking. That turned off some of the would-be tequila boozers.

That was a particularly rare kind of tequila called Mezcal. I remember it had a rough bite and I don't mean from the worm. I don't know where Leroy got it, but it certainly made an impression at the bar.

I even taught myself, with an empty bottle mind you, to spin the bottle as I tossed it into the air and caught it behind my back right before I poured the liquor. I thought such bartender tricks might impress some of the women. They didn't even look in my direction. And there were no cell phones in those days to distract them from observing the world around them. But my bottle tricks? Nothing.

One night, more than a year into my time at *Chez Haynes*, I finally got a few nights of work behind the bar. It was very exciting; even without a Norse goddess to show me the ropes of crafting *le cocktail parfait*. You had talked me through the basics of the Blue Lagoons and the Brandy Alexanders and Sidecars and a dozen more of the most popular drinks. Still, when I was finally let loose on my own, I knew next to nothing. American, Canadian, and British customers tended to know their cocktails well enough, and usually what they wanted. They could be tough. Ironically, the best client was the guy (almost always a man) who insisted on taking me step-by-step through a complicated concoction no one had ever heard of before. I also quickly learned that cocktails were clearly not the domain of the average Parisian. Back then, most of the French clientele had no clue. But they loved the idea of coming to an American restaurant, especially one with the soul and ambiance *Chez Haynes* provided, and that included a cocktail. It was part of *l'événement*. To them I was a maestro of the concoction by virtue of having a towel over my shoulder and a stainless-steel shaker in my hand. When I asked them what they wanted, they would say *'un cocktail'*. I would ask them which one they had in mind, and they would just say *'un cocktail, un cocktail'*" as if that was the name of the drink without any need of further description. I got into the habit of simply making them a Tequila Sunrise because it was easy to make, looked pretty with layers of color, a little paper umbrella, a cherry on a stick and a slice of orange on the rim. And the tequila made for a very pleasant evening all round. For many hundreds of Parisians in this speakeasy, *'un cocktail'* was a Tequila Sunrise and a Tequila Sunrise was *'un cocktail'*. My revenge for 'under the mountain'?

And then there were the drunks, the lushes, who came in to drink their supper as the saying goes. Most of them wanted to talk, and most of them were men, at least the ones who came to the bar. They spoke to me quite openly, and it was often dull and sad at the same time. And sometimes even embarrassing. I didn't dare give any advice. I was sure they just wanted to have a listener. By my listening they hopefully assumed that they were right about everything they recounted, especially the parts where they thought they had been 'done wrong', victimized I suppose is the correct word here.

I think these were the same guys who talked me through the crafting of their drinks. Often changing one cocktail for another as they ploughed their way through the evening on one of the bar stools. Lots of words. Occasionally even coherent. Often profane swear words. Too often. Even Leroy mentioned it. He probably swore as he did so. So, I cleaned out an old coffee can, took the label off and put the can on the bar under the lamp which sat on the corner. I told regulars they had to donate a franc every time they swore. It slowed down the swearing and gave us an extra income stream to put in the tip jar. The regulars thought it was funny. I would tell them 'The can is listening; you shouldn't defy the can'. Which soon became known as "the Great Can" or, as I came to refer to it, "the great Khan." Very quickly that morphed into 'Genghis Khan is listening'. And eventually to just "Genghis". Everyone soon knew who Genghis was, and they respected it. It went on for a few years, tempering the bar talk and, I like to think, raising our level of wit and fun. Genghis also raised quite a bit of loose change. Enough for an occasional Sunday dinner near the Odeon. *Vive Genghis!*

8.

The Switch

I HAVE NEVER POSSESSED THE gift of gab, and I was not one for small talk lasting hours and hours. I remember the first evening you came in with two beautiful women, you were talking a mile a minute, firing questions at me, and after a while you said to me, 'you don't talk much, do you?'.

I had forgotten the two other friends I was with. They were beautiful. Maybe that's why Leroy gave me the free beer. They were likely given wine, or cocktails.

In those days a bottle of wine a day was considered good for you, so the French invented the *crise de foie,* a made-up ailment for a hangover.

It was even a public health campaign. I had just arrived in Paris, and it immediately caught my attention. Every lamp post, kiosk and Metro billboard had a large poster attached asking Parisians to keep their wine consumption down to one bottle a day. It was an alcoholic-level target but, nevertheless, in Paris very stringent stuff. Then again, there were no posters about cocktail consumption. Or, for that matter, about drugs. Not that I witnessed. Certainly not by the look of some of the locals on the Rue Clauzel.

Leroy taught me the ropes, how to spot the junkies by their eyes. He once told me about Billie Holiday missing her heroin connection in the early fifties. He fed her yoghurt to get her through the night until her connection showed up in the early morning. Among the clients he pointed out were the high-class prostitutes, at five thousand francs a night, most were bilingual or trilingual, elegantly dressed in exquisite clothes, Dior, Yves Saint Laurent, Givenchy. Truth be told, I could never tell them apart, the wealthy *bourgeoises* and the expensive prostitutes. The guys they came in with were rarely as elegant. They were wealthy, rich, extrovert, often rude and crude, but the manageress put them in their place. Leroy also taught me to spot the heavies, the real estate goons up from Nice and the Côte d'Azur; these guys swaggered in and asked for Monsieur Leroy, and after a couple of times, Leroy told me they came to try to make him sell a large piece of land he owned near Nice. He had bought the property when he won the Irish Sweepstakes back in the fifties, and by now the land was worth millions. Leroy had turned his land into a nudist colony, and he liked to go down there in the summer and walk around buck naked.

Sometimes he walked around the restaurant buck naked. Or close to it. He would come in just wearing one of the large pink tee shirts he was always in. Like he simply forgot to put on the loose trousers he also perpetually wore. It was rare that he wore anything different. I used to wonder if he ever changed his clothes. Then one day I went up the street to his apartment to get a box of spices or something. He had clearly just done his laundry because hanging over two or three clothes lines stretching back and forth across his kitchen, he had hung up six or so identical pairs of freshly cleaned trousers and an equal number of meticulously washed large pink T-shirts. That pink T-shirt/easy trouser combo may have clashed with the 'haute couture' of many of his guests, but it was methodically assembled and worn every day. Except for those few days when the T-shirt came alone. The shirt never hung much lower than his waist so there would follow a short commotion as the manageress quickly ushered him back to the salad making station while one of the waitresses went back to his place to fetch the pair of trousers still waiting on the line.

Now, to get back to your work as the dishwasher and my job as the bartender.

You at your post and I at mine. Until...

You came out of the kitchen one evening and noticed that there were many people at the bar. You barged your way through and commented that maybe I should go back to the silence of the dishwashing tub in the kitchen, and you would handle the bartending. You loved to talk, and I didn't. So that's what we did off and on. I washed dishes, and you served drinks and chatted up the clients at the bar.

That is one version of 'the switch'. I will confess that people, the bar, the general hubbub always looked like a hugely fun party scene from my perspective. And I did like to engage. I don't remember the incident as me 'barging' so much as being permitted a minute breather to take in the fresh air and join the privilege of the bar. I desperately hoped my greasy T-shirt and the sweat still beading on my forehead was not a dead giveaway of my actual role and identity. (I was allowed, officially told, not to wear my wet apron in the dining area.) But that is not when or how 'the switch' happened. The origins of the switch happened when you, my friend, descended into my world. You came walking back to the kitchen underworld to use the toilet or looking for angostura bitters. After you had finished doing what you had to do, you looked in the kitchen, saw me alone, my hands, forearms, elbows and way too much of my biceps deep, deep, deep into the brown swill of the sink, and, I guess, you saw heaven. What I do remember is you walking up behind me, leaning forward and whispering in my ear:

You: 'You are so lucky, Greg.'

Me: 'What??'

You: 'You are so lucky, being back here.'

Me: 'How is that?'

You: 'By yourself. You don't have to talk to anyone. You can be alone.'

Me: 'Are you kidding me?'

You: 'No. I'd love it.'

Me: 'Really? If you want to switch, let's do it.'

So, we did. We talked to the manageress and Don. They thought you were out of your mind. But you were adamant that dishwashing was some kind of utopian existence that you were desperate to conceal yourself within. I think Don could not wait to get you back in the kitchen. He was positively delighted with the idea. Over the moon. And the manageress? Well maybe she had one or two scores to settle. Anyway, the next night we switched. I could not believe my luck. The universe had finally smiled on me.

And I was genuinely content communing with the greasy soap suds, listening to Don muttering about everything that was wrong with the world. It was a calming background voice, a human chirping. I wanted the silence of the dishwater. Making salads wasn't my passion, but it was a little like *bricolage*. And the only human sounds were from Don, cursing everything, and chuckling and cackling every so often. Saying a hundred times that timing was everything, in the kitchen and in life, and he'd intersperse his culinary philosophy with politics and how 'Hitler was damn efficient, the man knew what he was doing, getting rid of all that mixed blood', those were his words. Never for a moment seeing that he was pretty mixed himself, African American and Sicilian. Oh no, that never crossed his mind, at least not in the kitchen. After the racial stuff, Don would eventually get back to the manageress; now there was racial purity, blond and as Nordic as you can get, with a body to beat the band, he'd say.

So, we were both fully content with the new situation. Fair trade. Good swap. The switch of the century.

And there was also Don's running commentary about the waitresses coming in to pick up the food, how the girls waddled or sashayed or strutted their stuff. Don would cackle, slapping a greasy utensil against his apron. He was a good cook, all the customers agreed on that. I kept my mouth shut. I didn't want to antagonize the guy.

So, then, maybe it was not so perfect?

For all I knew his temper might explode and he'd grab me by the scruff of my neck and push my head down into the dishwater, and I'd hear 'is this what it feels like to fuck my blond girl? Huh?'

It all went extremely well for a few hours until Leroy came in. I could see he was in a temper of some kind—and not a good one—as he passed by the bar. He gave me a questioning look like something was out of place. Then he entered the kitchen and saw you. He immediately went into an angry rant. I could hear it from the bar. Don and Astrid trying to explain the idea to him. It was only for a night they were saying. He simmered down a fraction, but I could still hear his growl. I assumed it would be mere seconds before I was thrown back into my scullery solitude, or even out on the street. But then Leroy's mischievous side kicked in. He suddenly saw the humor and the sheer opportunity for drama. You and he making coffees and salads together. You and Don sharing stories. You suffering the depths of the sweat and the swill. Let the switch continue, he declared.

I don't remember much about making salads, just the lettuce leftovers which floated up in the dirty water once the plates had been prewashed. Lettuce will last forever I thought to myself, the other stuff disappeared, the carrots and tomatoes and onions and bits of eggs. The lettuce beat them all, drowned them, and in the water, the leaves took on all kinds of shadings, from dayglo to rust-brown. Lettuce must have been around with the dinosaurs. It's what they, the dinosaurs, ate that made them grow so big.

I do not know how to read this. Which are you? The onions or the lettuce?

Luckily for me, Leroy patrolled the kitchen frequently and kept Don in check.

Luckily for me, Leroy enjoyed this theatre as much as I did. How many weeks was it before you escaped the sink? Not nearly enough in my books, but the time I had at the bar was glorious. It gave me a taste of what was to come.

9.

Happiness

The Sunday dinners in the Latin Quarter, how can we forget them?

Sundays *Chez Haynes* was closed. Which was a break of sorts, but it meant finding somewhere else to eat our main meal of the day. Somewhere central. Somewhere cheap.

We looked around for a while, stopped outside the Chinese places and stared at the lit-up menu outside. And we found a place--*Le Paradis Mandarin*--- behind the Odéon metro station. Five francs, including bread and one Tsing Tao beer, and the bottles were bigger than the French ones.

It was a great deal. Even better than the eight Franc steak frites lunch specials in the cheaper cafes along the side streets of the Left Bank.

Sunday Chinese dinner became a ritual where we solved the world's problems, including those about art, women, love. We talked about theatre, you were also writing plays, along with your poetry. We discussed the theatre of the absurd at great lengths. Some Sundays we broke our rule of one beer only and went for two or three. This *paradis* was well-heated too, and that mattered in those wintery days.

I don't remember the one-beer rule unless it was because we couldn't afford it (which we couldn't) and didn't want to break the rule of law by running out on the bill. I do remember the talks about life and art and sex. I recall one evening casually throwing the concept of 'happiness' into the life-art-sex mix. You immediately reacted. Your head snapped back, and you looked at me like I had put a dog turd on your plate.

"Happiness?" you bellowed at me. "What has happiness got to do with anything?" I think I tried switching to a definition defense.

"Well, it depends on what you mean by happiness."

"No, it doesn't! Happiness has nothing to do with what we are doing here! In Paris."

It was almost as if 'happiness' was the enemy. Which maybe it was. Although we got a lot of laughter out of raising that incident over the years. I believe I half-heartedly ceded you this point. And then, over the years, I came to agree with it. Well, for the most part. Certainly, the very mention of it had made the bowl of noodles sitting before me in that little Chinese restaurant near the Odeon look sad and forlorn.

I sure sound like I was a pain in the ass sometimes, on my hifalutin high horse.

Not at all. It's what I needed.

Talk about dime store intellectual. Back to food. Outside *Chez Haynes*, I at least didn't eat too well.

'You at least'? You thought I was secretly feasting?

I wasn't interested in food. I was not and am not a gourmet. The glitzy food shops like Fauchon by the Madeleine and the fancy restaurants, I had no interest in them.

Mais, mon vieux, what about 'the *Paris-Brests, the pains aux raisins, the croissants aux amandes,* and the *congolais*'?

There were more important things in life for me, like love and children and human suffering and intellectual challenges. I had no idea about what nutritious food was, what was good or bad for me. Despite being in France, where everybody, and I mean everybody, usually went on and on about *la grande cuisine française*, I hated cooking; it was a waste of time, what with the chopping and the sautéing and the rigmarole of the spices. I didn't like shopping in the open-air markets either; the sellers asked me what I was going to cook, and I had no idea. I was just buying some vegetables, and when I asked for ground meat the *boucher* asked if it was *avec graisse*,, that is to say with fat for the dog or *sans graisse* for pasta or burgers, and I would say I'm the dog, look at me, don't I look like a healthy dog? And she would laugh with some bewilderment in her eyes.

The ground meat for the dog was the cheapest. There were many days early on when I dreamed of a meal with meat, even *'avec graisse'*. I didn't bark or anything, but I would have rolled over.

And in the supermarkets, I would simply walk down the aisle with my basket and grab the stuff off the shelves, pasta, rice salt, olive oil, canned this and canned that. I didn't inspect every item for the best price. A can of beans is a can of beans, how much could the price difference be? I rarely bought potatoes because I'd forget about them and before I knew it the spuds would sprout hairy warts under the sink. The truth was that I rarely cooked at all. I nearly always ate on the move, in the street.

Street food was delicious but not always affordable. *'Frites'* usually were. I loved potatoes. Now I call them 'carbs' but back then they were a staple. I think I rivalled you for lack of knowledge and enthusiasm for the complexities of flavor which Paris celebrated. Remember Thomas? Mid-west Thomas? He was studying to be a chef at *Le Cordon Bleu Paris*. One day he showed up to work in the kitchen with Don for a few months. I think he needed an internship for his studies and Leroy was a sucker for people in need. In addition, Thomas needed a place to stay. I told him about the empty *chambre de bonne* on my floor. That *chambre* had a built-in shower. He was totally into flavor and made some amazing food for his school assignments which he would bring back and share. I remember one evening he was describing the different ingredients and recipes he was working with at some length. After ten or fifteen minutes, I finally interrupted him and said "it all sounds great, Thomas, but you are talking to the wrong guy. At this stage in my life, when it comes to food, I just look for grease and bulk." He was horrified. "Grease and bulk!!" he shrieked back. He cared deeply about food, and I had just 'knifed' him. Metaphorically.

What I cared about was painting and having money to buy canvas and paints and books. I wanted to own the books I read. I don't know why. I rarely used the public libraries in Paris. I've kept all the books. I never bought stretchers for the canvases though, they were so expensive; I stapled the canvas to the wall and painted, and when I was done, and the canvas had dried, I rolled up the work and stored it in a corner. Art historians never talk about storage problems for painters, but after a year of painting on stretched canvases, the unsold pieces—-and that always meant everything you painted——took up a lot of room. The point was to paint, not to stretch and prime the canvas in order to paint. I wasn't picky about where I painted, I didn't need good natural light. A good painting could hold its own under any kind of light. Diego Velazquez holds up perfectly well in the basement by candlelight or on a terrace by bright sunlight. I didn't need the right music either. I have known painters who just had to have music, the right kind of music, their special kind of music. Who could afford a decent sound system anyway? Just turn on the radio, which I did later when I acquired a little one, a Telefunken I think it was. You get more variety on the radio anyway, even if the French love talking on the music programs.

I remember we debated the practical differences between painting and writing. You complained about the money it cost to paint. The canvas, the paint, the tools, the storage, the actual space to lay a canvass down and swing a brush. Writers just needed paper and a pen (or typewriter) and a desk. I agreed but I also pointed out that after you had completed your toil, you had a finished work, ready to go to market—which in your case soon became the many bona fide galleries in which you exhibited. After I finished with paper and pen, there was no finished product. Just paper with words on it—and the hope of a publisher or producer to finish it off. And finish it off they usually did. Which is why we found alternatives. Not that it mattered. The money was not there either way. Although, usually enough to buy a pen.

Yeah, I spent money on essentials for painting, and essentials for clothes. And food. Except for Sundays when you and I splurged on Chinese food and Tsing Tao beer. Sometimes two beers, my friend.

Yes, we did have that. And, as you reminded me, 'happiness' was not important anyway.

10.

Names and Nightmares

As far as money goes, *Chez Haynes* wasn't cheap, and the 'names' who frequented the restaurant were well off. One of these names was the writer James Baldwin who often came into the restaurant at a quarter to two in the morning, just before we closed. He was a pal of Leroy, who had also known the writer and poet Richard Wright who had died in Paris under murky circumstances. Baldwin sometimes arrived late at night, with the African American painter Beauford Delaney. We, the staff, were supposed to go home at two. We were all tired. But Leroy knew we would stay as long as necessary for Baldwin.

He didn't need to insist too hard. Staying open for Baldwin was never a chore.

You're right. Baldwin was a great man.

I knew of him from a book I read in high school English class—*Go Tell it on the Mountain*. But at that time, I didn't get the significance. It was just another book, like *Othello*, which I had to read. I don't know if they were for the same class, I just know I read them. But in university, before I came to Paris, Baldwin's name often came up in late night conversations and/or at Anti-Vietnam and Civil Rights gatherings. So, he was a 'name'.

Even a 'star', but I do not remember anyone talking about him like that. That would have been too flimsy a descriptor. Not that *Chez Haynes* didn't attract its share of celebrities and so-called 'stars' of the day: Paloma Picasso, Jacques Dutronc, Isabelle Adjani, Johnny Hallyday.

Oh yes, I remember Paloma, she used to come in with her boyfriend and she always paid by check, so I knew her address in Neuilly. I never asked her if she spoke Spanish. I never even told her I admired her father. I was struck by her stark beauty. What could I say? Flirt with her in Spanish?

James Baldwin was in a different league entirely. It was as if Sartre or Beckett had walked in. Which neither ever did; not in the four years I haunted the place. But Baldwin did. Sartre died near the end of my time in Paris. There was a huge turnout for his funeral. So maybe he had an excuse. But Beckett lived on for another ten years--no excuse. I remember Baldwin as being rather relaxed and cool. The epitome of 'cool'. That kind of cool that is laced through and through with brilliance. You must remember when I first saw him, I was just the kid in the back. I didn't even know he was there for an hour. I was cleaning out the sink or tidying up the salad station, wiping down the espresso machine. Then I was called out of the kitchen for a few minutes to fetch something from the bar. The restaurant was almost empty but suddenly it was host to an amazing seminar--and for a moment I got to slow walk through it and listen to James Baldwin up close say words, any words. His voice was enough itself.

Sometimes one of the waitresses, Sophia, if I remember right, brought some cocaine, and we would snort up in the WC. Full of energy, the staff would now be turbo-charged, attending to Baldwin and Beauford quickly and efficiently. Baldwin would complement Leroy on the service and how energetic the staff were so late at night. Leroy may have suspected something, and now that I think back, I'm sure he knew that we were on some good high suddenly. There was a twinkle in his eye as he kidded Baldwin, telling him that the staff, all aspiring artists of one kind or another, admired him. And we did. He was unpretentious, something so rare among successful creative people. Especially painters--they were the worst in their boasts and incessant bragging about their own shows and their name-dropping was sickening.

That kind of 'big-boast-small-talk' used to drive you crazy, especially at an art show: yours, theirs, whosever. The talk became ridiculous. It betrayed a particular poverty of thinking that all communities are prey to. Especially those where self-identity as artist or writer was still precarious. You would seethe, then suddenly announce you were bored (your favorite word when you were annoyed and uneasy) and leave. It is amazing the depth of emotion which the words of peers can elicit. I wish I could say I was immune. But none of us are. I tend to respond with foolish jokes.

Responding with a joke is smart. Baldwin and Beauford would invite Leroy to sit with them, and they'd shoot the breeze for a while. They'd invite him to a drink or two.

They shared a common community. Sitting around the pink clothed tables of the restaurant late into the night. I envied them that. But they also shared a common nightmare. It's no wonder Leroy drank.

Leroy smoked weed too and hash once in a while, and he could afford as much cocaine as he wanted, but Leroy's high of predilection was scotch and could he put it away. I knew because as the bartender, I not only brought up the wine bottles and the beer cases from the *cave*, but I also replenished the hard stuff. Every evening when I got to work, I refilled near-empty bottles on the mirror shelves behind the bar. I knew how full the bottles had been when I had left the bar the previous evening. The only person who had access to the liquor was Leroy. It was quite shocking the amount of scotch Leroy drank after hours.

That moment behind the bar at the beginning of the night would frequently signal what kind of night it would be. When I finally took over the bar full time, apart from the single malts, I remember there being three bottles of whisky lined up together on that mirrored shelf. A bottle of J&B, a bottle of Ballantine's and a bottle of Johnnie Walker Red. At the end of the night, when we closed up, they were still mostly full. We filled them up regularly. I can't remember which one Leroy started with, but the next evening would usually begin by me letting the waitresses know if it was a one, two or three bottle night we were facing. If it was the latter, we often didn't see him, so those nights were a crapshoot. To give Leroy his due, on many nights (and there were many) there was no whisky missing. It was an on-going war he was in; one he knew all too well, and some days the battles were won and other days they were not.

When he'd see me bringing up the new bottles, he'd say 'hey Rafael, who the hell is drinking my liquor? You guys drinking on the job or what?' Toward the end of the evening when he was good and loose, he'd talk about the African American writers and poets, and Langston Hughes and Chester Himes.

Those were insights which the bottle brought us care of Leroy. He paid the price of admission for all of us. Sometimes the price was darker and unexpected. Even on his drinking nights he could give a sharp and sober critique of America. The amusing incident, the funny remark on growing up in the U.S. turned sour. A whisky sour of a different kind. Crude, angry, bitter. One of the American waitresses once asked him how he could be so hard on his own country. 'You're American', she said. His eyes flashed and he just said, 'Baby, I was never American', and he walked back into the kitchen. We all knew what he meant. Even if we didn't know. Even if we didn't have the faintest idea of what it was like, what it truly felt like.

He told us he was writing a book about the black experience in Berlin during the war. He mentioned this oeuvre quite a few times. I found it intriguing, to say the least. We knew he'd been in Berlin after WWII, he knew the German capital, and I think his heart went out to the few blacks who had been caught in the Nazi horrors and had survived. I asked myself why he never asked Baldwin for help in getting the book published. Africans trapped in the Hitlerian hellish maelstrom were a tragic subject. The Africans in Berlin were referred to in later years as the Rhineland Bastards. German soldiers had been in Angola, when it was a German colony, until 1914, they had children with the local women and some of the offspring came to Germany.

I don't think he ever finished the book. I am not sure he wanted to. I remember him showing me some of the pages one day. They were good. He clearly had testimony to give and a story to tell. But it was a hard story to tell. He alluded to it sometimes, but not in much detail. I do remember one slow night back at the salad station he told me he had started a PhD after college. He was sitting on his chair peeling onions or potatoes. I think he said the PhD was in sociology. Early in the process he went back to the small town where he had been raised—in Kentucky I think—to research the local archives the year he was born. At that time, he said, they listed the town population as '635 people and 847 cows, pigs and n****rs.' I am guessing here at the numbers. He may also have been guessing when he told me. But that, of course, was not the point. 'I was lumped in the second group', he said quietly, never looking up from the bucket of peels. I am assuming it was sometime afterwards that he joined the American army. Then he went to war. After it ended, he never went back. Despite all the stories about his life, he was rarely forthcoming about the overt racism that asphyxiated his existence. Not to us. It would have been good to read more pages. It would not have been an easy read. Clearly it was not an easy write.

Once I went to Leroy's apartment to get some papers, and there in his living room, I saw ten chapters nailed to the wail, not stapled or in folders; no, he had driven a three-inch nail through the pages of each chapter as if to emphasize the brutality of that era. I couldn't help thinking of the spikes smashed into the twisted, deformed hands of Christ in Grünewald's *Crucifixion rétable* in Colmar in France. At the time, I had only seen the painting in reproduction. Years later, I drove to Colmar and looked at that stunning work, and my mind went back to Leroy's book and the chapters nailed to the wall. After he died, his belongings disappeared, there were rumors that the novel was going to be published, but nothing ever came of it. I don't even know if the pages still exist. Maybe Leroy destroyed them. It was the kind of thing he might do. I also think at times that the U.S. government made sure some of his things disappeared. Leroy had been in army intelligence after all. He said it himself more than once. You don't fuck with the Internal Revenue Service and you sure as hell don't fuck with the U.S. Army.

11.

Dieu me pardonnera. C'est son métier.

You knew about dishwashing because you worked in the kitchen, and you also made salads.

As life skills go, I could have done worse.

And, as mentioned, I too, spent some weeks back in the kitchen with my hands deep in dishwater after we traded jobs. I was fed up with talking to the drunks at the bar, and you who have a knack for entertaining people with talk, wanted to try bartending. You could learn something new. It is, after all, a useful *métier.*

As a *métier*, bar tending did come in handy. Who doesn't have to deal with drunks from time to time? It served me well later also, after I left Paris for London. Kept me alive for a few more years. It left the day open for writing and fed and entertained me in the evening. For a couple of months, it even provided a pub roof under which to sleep. As *métiers* go it is far down the list from that in Heine's Parisian death bed whisper—*Dieu me pardonnera. C'est son métier*, which hung above my desk in Paris for many years—but sweeter than the sink.

Conversation was your thing as they say, plus you wrote plays. You knew something about dialogue.

Much of bartending at *Chez Haynes* was about words, about the conversation, the 'crack' as the Irish say. It was also about theatre. The place was dressed like a stage and there were people coming and going, making their entrances and exits all through the night. With just a comment thrown in here and there, suddenly there was a real entertainment. And the restaurant's reputation allowed for it. From the moment people entered. You will remember the barman was responsible for taking reservations. The phone rang as soon as we arrived for work and continued most of the evening. Over and over, we would answer the phone and say exactly the same thing: *"Chez Haynes. Bonsoir"*. It was ingrained in our heads. So much so that even on our day off it haunted us. I remember the night that I call 'tequila night' almost as much for your morning greeting as for the night itself. But more of that later.

I sometimes asked myself: Was this my new identity? *Chez Haynes*? As identities go it wasn't bad. Now, in geezer-hood I am still trying to figure that one out. Finding myself, I mean. I know this is coming from left field, but before we started this dialogue we said, if it's important to one of us, well, we'll talk about it, now, here.

Absolutely.

I don't want to find myself. Guys who find themselves tend to be boring. Suddenly you know yourself, you have an opinion on everything, you've found yourself. That's a euphemism, usually for he's got character, which is another euphemism for he's a fucking bore.

I doubt either of us has ever been accused of having 'character'. Not the respectable kind. Maybe of playing a character or two. And not always for the good. For me taking a '*Chez Haynes*' reservation was a good moment for distraction and entertainment. When I asked the caller when and what name the reservation was for, they would give me the date and time (usually that same evening) and their name—*Monsieur Badeaux*, or whatever. I would ask them to hold a moment, then come back to them and say, I am sorry, but I am unable to take a reservation tonight for anyone whose name begins with a B. Maybe tomorrow night or later in the week. They were usually astounded and would say something like '*Mais, c'est pas possible. C'est fou!*' and I would explain that it was worth more than my job to go against my patron's wishes. He is eccentric, believes in a kind of *égalité de réservation par alphabet*. Most of our Parisian customers knew enough of the Leroy myth to accept that this might possibly be true. It was an American restaurant after all. Soul food. Unusual, by definition. I would then ask if they could give me a name with a different first letter and after another moment of '*c'est fou*', they would give me another name, say Gagneux, and I would confirm that G worked for that day. Later, in the evening when they arrived at our door, I would ask if they had a reservation and they would say '*Oui, pour Monsieur Gagneux*'. I would look at our reservation book, flip a few pages, then look back at them and say 'I'm sorry we have no reservation for *Gagneux*' for this evening. They would either begin to protest or just look at me disbelieving. At which point I would say we do, however, have a reservation for a Monsieur Badeaux. There usually followed a silent wide-eyed '*c'est vraiment fou*'. Mercifully, every time I did this, nobody protested further or got angry. Unusual for Parisians. But after a second, most laughed. Cheerfully. They were relieved and often shared the joke with their dinner party. As if it was all part of the experience of this strange restaurant up at the top of the ninth *arrondissement*, just shy of the most famous red-light district in Europe. I like to believe the relief made their evening more fun, and I am certain I sold more wine.

Nowadays you'd get fired, for pulling such a stunt. Everyone is way too sensitive these days about such things. Political correctness gone haywire.

Possibly. But as correctness goes, political correctness has always looked preferable to traditional correctness which has a brutal legacy of inequity and coercion. I continued my hoax for a few months, once or twice a night, and not with expats, always with Parisians. The regulars at the bar caught on as did the waitresses and they all played along. I don't think Leroy knew. He never mentioned it. Although I like to think he would have appreciated the sheer theatricality of the moment.

Another thing I remember well was that when the waitresses didn't like some of the clients, they gave them double-dose strong coffee when they asked for decaf. When the clients asked if this decaf was for real, the waitresses took on a surprised look. They'd say, 'oh yes siree, we have this very special decaf for the espresso machine, fantastic stuff, no caffeine at all, but it tastes exactly like real coffee', and the client would shut up. Once back in the kitchen, the waitress would mumble 'that'll show the cocksucker.' And Don would add, 'you show 'em, girl.'

Revenge theatre. (Just one of the many 'theatres' that invaded Paris back then.) Nevertheless, like any good theatre, there were lots of moments where the audience had to suspend belief. Maybe, it wasn't always a decaf, maybe the leaves of lettuce were not always perfectly fresh, and maybe the Norse goddess sometimes insisted the barely touched potato salad or the rice (minus the Gauloise ash) be recycled from one plate to the next. The ambiance was still the same. It was an American restaurant in Paris. If anything, I think it added a touch of authenticity. Besides, *'Dieu nous pardonnera. C'est son métier.'*

12.

Des leçons d'amour

Remember that evening, when you were still making salads, and I asked you to slip a folded note under the lettuce? From the bar I had seen these two couples come in with an unaccompanied, elegantly dressed, young woman. The waitress placed them at table five. I asked the waitress serving them to remember the salad the single woman ordered. I went back to you in the kitchen, and said, 'Greg, slip this in her salad, it's a note I wrote to her'.

I remember you being very interested in this woman. Instantly obsessed. We ran through a few scenarios. You suggested I tell her you liked her if she came back to use the toilet. I suggested you serve the wine at her table and so on. The note idea came as we were talking at the salads station. You hesitated for a moment, then wrote it out. Fortunately, she ordered a salad and Laura passed on the information. Just a short note under the lettuce. I think I slipped it between two pieces of lettuce which were at the bottom of the salad––two base leaves on which the main salad was served. Pretty straight forward.

By the time the young woman started eating the salad, the staff knew all about my note. We were all staring at the woman as she ate her salad. Soon she'll come across my *billet-doux*, I thought, open it, and look at me behind the bar. In the message I had asked if she'd like to have a drink later. But nothing doing. As we watched, she ate and ate--the whole damn salad, including my piece of paper. The waitresses were laughing.

The plate came back clean. There was no note on the floor or left on the table. Sometimes customers did not eat the lettuce, but she evidently had. We assumed she had rolled the leaves and the note together and eaten it all at the same time. It was the best working theory we had. But who knows?

These customers paid their bill, and as they passed the bar on their way out, I leaned forward toward the woman and said:

"Do you know there was a note from me in your salad, and you ate it. You didn't even see it, let alone read it".

She stopped, looked at me, and said:

"That's one of the best come-on lines I've ever heard, but the answer is still no."

"Why not?" I asked. She turned to her friends who were already at the door and said to them "I'll be right with you". Then she turned back to me and added, "do you really think I'd go out with you?"

"Well, yes," I said.

"Look again," she said, "you look like a nice young man." She leaned forward across the bar, her breasts showing just enough. She beckoned I come closer and then she said quietly, in perfect unaccented English, "don't you see? The two guys are getting rid of the two bimbos, and I'm taking both johns to a very expensive hotel."

"Which hotel? Can I meet you there later," I asked?

"Don't be a fool," she said. "I make in one night what you make in two months." She waved at me from the door, but she didn't wink. She couldn't have been more than thirty.

Heart break is part of the deal when you work in a restaurant. Especially if you fall in love with a prostitute. They are way too smart to 'date' a penniless barman or dishwasher. No matter how much we thought our good looks, deep personality, future fame would be enough. The only time any kind of money was exchanged on my behalf for a prostitute did not come out of my pocket. One of our regulars, Quentin, an Englishman from Sussex, suggested we go out for a drink after *Chez Haynes* closed. He wanted to take a closer look at one of the late-night bars up around the corner closer to Pigalle. More than curious, I was happy to tag along so long as he was paying the bill, which he was.

Immediately upon entering I could see that the prices were out of my league. Not even close. Quentin bought an exceptionally overpriced bottle of Champagne, (certainly over 500F, a month's rent). The deal was that we paid for the bottle, and two of the bar's lovely 'hostesses' would sit and 'talk' to us as we drank, kindly refraining from taking more than a sip or two. Quentin was very specific about the woman he wanted to 'talk' to. He was very keen to converse with an African French hostess. I was very happy with the young woman who stepped forward and smiled at me. Quentin paid for the bottle, and they led us to a secluded table in a back corner. Of course, even a bottle of champagne didn't get you very far. So, the evening became an interesting game of them exchanging introductory kisses, fondling, and fumbling for the opportunity to negotiate another bottle of champagne and/or sell us the supreme package, which involved taking us to a room in the back for more involved play. Quentin seriously contemplated it, but ultimately declined. It was an easy choice for me as I did not have any money. My 'date' had clearly figured that out long before I told her. Nevertheless, she kept to her side of the bargain.

The prostitutes I talked to at *Le Trafalgar* up the street were not in the same league, clearly, but they were often educated. I asked them about their *métier*, and they were straightforward about it. Fifteen minutes, a hundred francs, in a small hotel room nearby, rented by the month or maybe longer, I suppose. One of the women called her room her *bureau, h*er office. And she told me she was an ex-schoolteacher, ex-*institutrice*. What did you talk about?

We had a conversation about writing. She didn't write but she liked poetry, which I thought was kind of her to say. I think I even recited one of my shorter poems. Given her English, I don't believe she fully followed it; even less so when I tried explaining it in French. But she nodded appreciatively, which also went well beyond what she was reasonably expected to do. Later, of course, I realized she would have been adept at listening to client's stories, boasts, grievances, regrets, and poems. Although, I don't think I figured that out until the next night, back behind the *Chez Haynes* bar, listening to Quentin's regret at not paying to go to the back room with his hostess.

'She was beautiful. I should have bought a second bottle', he grumbled.

'Another beer?' I asked him.

He nodded. I slid a fourth or fifth Heineken towards him. He paid, but I didn't have to go into the backroom with him. I did have to listen to his regrets for another hour, plus a little bit of swearing, followed by the jingle of a few coins tossed into Genghis.

I didn't know how to react to the high-class call girl who ate my note, and I probably blushed. Leroy, ever observant, came over to the bar and said:

"Her name is Sarah. I don't know what she told you. But you can't afford her. Nor can I. When she was starting out, she gave me a freebie once in a rare while because I would give her and her clients the royal treatment here, and her high rollers appreciated it. They liked the exotic Southern atmosphere. And get this, she used to be a professor of philosophy at the Sorbonne."

"What?" I blurted out.

"Yeah," Leroy continued, "can you picture it? In a Sorbonne amphitheater, teaching all those snot-nosed, existentially angst-ridden students with enough wood between their legs for New York Yankees baseball bats."

I cannot recall my companion's name and I'm sure she forgot mine the minute Quentin and I left the bar. But she was very pretty, very sweet, and about my age. In another life, maybe? I wonder.

Leroy never mentioned Sarah again to me, but once in a while when some clients came in, he'd come to the bar and would say 'that one's like Sarah'. After a few weeks he'd just give me a nod.

Never too old, or young, to receive *des leçons d'amour*.

13.

Pig Alley and the Theatre of the Street

PIGALLE. IT ALWAYS AMAZED ME that *Chez Haynes* was so close to this pinnacle of the Parisian night. You would never know just by going to the restaurant. Going to work every night, getting off the metro at the *St Georges* station, and walking the few minutes to the restaurant was a quiet experience. A few blocks from all the lights and traffic and people, Rue Clauzel was a dark, empty street back then. Most likely still is. A very discrete location. I suspect many, if not most of our American clients booked dinner with us followed by a tour of Pigalle. It was a must see on most tourist itineraries.

One night, I remember hearing loud American voices on the street outside the restaurant. A table of three or four had just left the restaurant and now they were outside the front door, upset about something. Suddenly, one of them swept back in through the red curtains and saloon doors and looked up at me and demanded directions to Pigalle, which she pronounced in a sharp New York accent as 'Pig Alley'. 'Where is Pig Alley?' she demanded. 'I didn't come all this way to miss Pig Alley.' She turned to her friends, who had followed her in and were all nodding and saying, 'Pig Alley'. I gave her directions and off they went. We all laughed about their pronunciation, but in many ways, it was an apt description of the place.

What that woman didn't know was that Pigalle was a famous eighteenth-century sculptor. He did a sitting portrait of Voltaire in his birthday suit. And it seems Voltaire liked it. The statue is in the Louvre. The sex den of Paris named after a sculptor--only in Paris. Pigalle also had the Hermes statue on top of the Bastille column.

Sex, art, and revolution all rolled into one.

Terrific, *pourquoi pas*? I wonder if Voltaire was a *chaud lapin*, a hot rabbit.

A hot rabbit in pig alley. Good juxtaposition of images. What is a hot rabbit?

A horny rabbit.

I shouldn't have asked.

When *Chez Haynes* closed at two in the morning, the staff would walk up to *Le Trafalgar* to unwind. The clients and the prostitutes at *Le Trafalgar* situated off the Rue Blanche, were different from the *poules de luxe,* expensive prostitutes or escorts who came to *Chez Haynes.*

Deluxe chickens, now? This area is beginning to sound more like a farmyard than a seedy red-light district.

The place was an unpretentious, old-fashioned brasserie, with a zinc bar, Formica tables and chairs, and tired waiters.

It was a very cool bar. We were off the beaten track but somehow right in the middle of this amazing slice of Paris nightlife. I am not sure I fully appreciated it at the time. It was just a place we hung out.

Monsieur Xavier, the owner, always greeted us warmly. He had a protruding belly and a curly moustache. The first night we went there he told us he was from Normandy and would always be thankful to the American soldiers who saved France. He had been a young lad then as he watched the Americans after D-Day rumble through the town in their armored vehicles. And some nights when he was a bit soused, he'd puff out his chest and rattle off the famous beaches of Operation Overlord, Juno, Gold, Sword, Omaha, and Utah. The late-night customers at *Le Trafalgar* were the real fauna of Pigalle-by-night: cops on a break from their beat, flower sellers not selling anything, prostitutes, not selling anything either, musicians resting their feet from their playing in a few bars and restaurants. Most of the year the musicians played outside on the terraces, and now as fall moved into winter it would soon be too cold to play in the street, and most restaurants didn't want the musicians playing inside. The *accordéonistes*, guitar and violin players would leave Paris for the south soon, heading for the *midi* and the sun. As Aznavour sang, *La misère est moins pénible au soleil;* misery is less painful in the sun.

They had the right idea. We should have followed their lead.

And the cops never bothered us about our identity papers there either. They all knew we were from *Chez Haynes*. The cops chatted with everybody pretty much, and the prostitutes were usually in a good mood. I asked the prostitutes about the *maquereaux*, the pimps, and the women said they were independent, they weren't making that much money anyway. The atmosphere in the bar was out of a Jules Maigret scene. I've always liked Simenon. He writes simple prose, deceptively easy to read and the stories are intriguing and psychologically tense. I think he's a great writer.

Time for a confession. I am ashamed to say that when you first mentioned Maigret to me back then, I thought you were talking about Magritte, the surrealist painter—whom you had probably schooled me about a few days earlier. He (the artist) might have appreciated the juxtaposition. Master of the unconventionally odd and, I later learned, alleged forger of bank notes and paintings when times were tough, or projects needed to be funded. I can fully sympathize, especially, as much of it happened during the Nazi occupation of Belgium when subversion and resistance were all the rage. And one's physical life depended on it. Getting into trouble then was a lot different than getting into trouble on the fringes of Pigalle in 1976.

We only ran into trouble once, remember? One evening after we left *Le Trafalgar*. We walked down a small street off Rue des Martyrs. I forget the name of the alley. We saw three young men stumbling toward us. Their voices were loud. I could understand that they were insulting us, calling us *sales américains* and *pauvres cons, on va casser de l'amérloque ce soir*, we're going to give them a lesson, eh, *alors les gars*? I told you that the guys intended to beat the crap out of us, *les amerloques*, then and there.

At least they were not wearing Gestapo uniforms and carrying submachine guns.

And then you walked right up to them and started shouting at them. "Who the fuck do you think you are, you cock-suckers? Get the fuck out of here, you wanna fight, you miserable shits?" You put on quite a show there, these kids had seen too many American movies, and they understood the rough talk, especially the word *fuck*. They stepped back, and you went right on. "You lily-livered freaks, you wanna fight, eh? You wanna rumble? Well, come on, we're ready, you dumb assholes! Come on motherfucker! Try me! Go on, try me!" By this time, you were screaming at them, right in their faces, and they backed off, then turned and walked away, looking furtively back. That was Pigalle theatre too, eh?

Sounds more like 'Pig Alley' theatre. I don't remember sounding quite so crazy. But I am not fully denying it. We were into all kinds of theatrical experiments back then. If I recall clearly (and I don't) I think those guys were pretty young. Even younger than me. But there were quite a few of them. Fortunately, I did not understand much of what they were saying. I do not consider myself stupid, not to the point of physical harm stupid, so maybe I thought we could count on the cops back in the bar if things went askew. I do remember not feeling frightened. But then, I never felt any real street fear in Paris. We could go anywhere any time of day or night. I may have assumed that the street kids and gangs were not as violent as American, or even British, street kids. I was undoubtably wrong, but not having seen any films with French gangs doing violence on the street (I am sure there were plenty), I foolishly assumed these young men were mostly bark. So, we just needed to bark louder. And that episode was the perfect experiment to test out the theory. That time it worked. I never tried it again. Not even when drunk and arguing with a taxi driver. Which I did a few times.

What a performance! I'd never heard the expression 'lily-livered' before. Did you make that up on the spot? Great acting there, my friend.

The expression 'lily-livered' or 'yellow-bellied' came from a movie I saw. A western. I think it was a line John Wayne said in more than one of his films. But you are right, it was just performance theatre. Which I enjoyed. We would try things out on street audiences all the time. One of my favorites was up on the Boulevard Strasbourg with Stephen. I think it was during the time we were rehearsing *One Day in May*. What we were doing there I do not remember. I think the rehearsal space we found was nearby. Anyway, several of us were walking along the street, and Stephen had this white cane and old hat and began miming a blind man. He was tapping the cane in front of him down the sidewalk to the intersection of Strasbourg with another large street. I pretended to be a concerned citizen and went up to him and asked him if I could help him. He said yes, and I took his arm and began walking him across the street. Halfway across, there was a median strip with a large metal lamp post on it. As we approached it, I deliberately walked him into it. Stephen had this great theatrical trick of furtively throwing his hand out at waist height and slapping the lamppost at the same time as his head brushed the lamppost. The loud thump and the sudden snapping back of his head made it look and sound as if he had genuinely smacked his head extremely hard into the lamppost. It worked perfectly. And I laughed. But we had not anticipated the reaction of the Parisians out on the Boulevard that day. Some had been watching the whole sequence and were absolutely horrified that I had deliberately walked a blind man into a lamp post for my own amusement.

I can't help laughing out loud here. It's just the kind of humor you loved.

You were particularly vulnerable to slapstick. Anyway, the anger on the street was so palpable and livid and quick that without mentioning it to each other, we instantly both knew that confessing to a theatrical prank would not go over well. I immediately dashed across the rest of the avenue; a cascade of abuse hurled at me as I made off into a side street. Stephen had to play the scene out, explaining he was all right. Unhurt. They walked him the other half of the way across, and he persuaded them he was fine to walk off on his own. We caught up later to debrief. The incident did teach me a lesson about street theatre. You cannot drop your act if you are not letting the audience into the fact that they are an audience. It was not a prank show.

I used that lesson in the theatre course which I taught at the American Center on Boulevard Raspail. In class, I stressed realism in performing. I remember saying something to the effect that acting is not so much the addition of tricks and deceits as it was the shedding of the unnatural behaviors provoked by having an audience in front of you. It was my kind of 'method' philosophy at the time. To engage in this authentically (that was a big word at the time), we would often go out into public spaces and perform pre-developed, semi-improvised scenes. I insisted the students had to play it through no matter what happened. They were evoking real responses in the audience which they had to be careful not to mock by letting on it was all pretend. Paradoxically, they needed to shed any desire to 'perform' and stay themselves.

The only other time the 'audience' reacted as intensely as on that day on the Boulevard Strasbourg was in the metro. On *Ligne 4*. The metro was a great place to develop a resistance to the inclination to 'perform'. There was a ready-made relatively fixed audience, used to day-to-day incidents, like Wendy's univited assault. But also, a multitude of musicians and performers walking through the carriages, peddling their artistic wares. So, I figured a little concealed theatre should not be particularly unsettling.

Talk about a captive audience. I never knew about these theatrical workshops in the metro.

I recall you taking part in some of the workshops at the American Center. I don't think it was your favorite experience. When you were in an intense scene or exercise, you would jump up, saying 'I'm bored'. Then you would sit down and continue, just to jump up a few minutes later and again say 'I'm bored'. I never knew dramatic tension could be so deadly tedious. Afterwards, you said you would stick to set design. Which was best as I am not sure shouting 'I'm bored,' would have worked well in the metro. Although there might have been much agreement.

I find all this fascinating. And gee, Greg, I always thought I was a wonderful actor, and here you tell me I was an asshole.

Not an asshole. Just an honest critic. A typical Paris metro-based scene was usually simple, but the set-up took some preparation. In one instance, at a pre-ordained station two actors, a man, and a woman in their thirties, got on the train and sat down together. They were to behave like new lovers, holding hands, cuddling, saying sweet things to one another, kissing. Not so unusual in Paris. The audience quickly got it. There were some shared looks and smiles, some glanced away but after a short time, they were the center of attention in that section of the train. Even commuters who entered at a later stop got the picture. About five stations later, the woman rose to leave with a final kiss and promises to meet the man later. Just as she left the metro car, waving back at him, another 'actor', a similarly aged woman entered the train car. She was the man's 'wife'. She saw the first woman leave and wave. Then she saw her 'husband'. She was not initially upset, just surprised to see him. He was supposed to be at work or with the children—I cannot remember the details. Then it slowly dawned on her, and she asked who the woman was. He lied and told her she was a colleague or some such thing. The 'wife' never got very upset or angry but kept probing his answers. Eventually, his lies became so exaggerated and defensive, even nasty, that some of the 'audience' members felt they had to intervene. Suffice it to say that he too was forced to exit hastily. The 'wife' travelled on a few more stops with some others in the carriage telling her what had transpired in full detail, one woman even insisting she divorce him. All she could do was nod her head until the next stop where she and I (a very quiet observer) exited. You do not drop out of character in such situations. It was not a gag. Just a class scene. We likely broke all kinds of unwritten ethical protocols. I sometimes wonder how far this work was from Wendy's unprovoked incident with her mother on the metro. But it was a different time. The time of 'Pig Alley'. We were always sliding along the edge of ethical protocols of one sort or another.

14

Celebrity and the WC

Movie stars and singers came to *Chez Haynes.* French stars of the sixties and seventies. Most of them were polite.

Yes, most of them. But they were even more polite when I worked at the bar. There were not many lengthy conversations back by the kitchen.

'Toilette?'

'Là, monsieur.' I point to the door of the little WC just off the kitchen.

'Merci.'

Although the *'merci'* was more of an option which some did not feel was worth the price of civility.

I learned quite a bit about famous people, from the way they treated the bartender. The ones who were polite were relaxed, I could sometimes tell just by the way they moved or sat at the bar waiting for the staff to prepare their table--that they were at ease in their skin, as the French expression goes, *bien dans leur peau.* Some of these stars were fidgety, and rarely said please when they ordered a drink or a cocktail. What always surprised me was that they still felt the need to name-drop, either directly to me or making sure to chat loudly enough with their friends so others could easily overhear.

Like we are doing in this book.

Okay. Maybe. But we're not famous. Other celebrities were easy-going and polite. Warren Beatty was reading *Ten Days That Shook the World,* when he came in, and he said a few words to me about the book. Later, at his table, he was not in a rush when he ordered.

And a definite *'merci'* when directed to the toilet.

One of the waitresses, Laura I think, spent the following weekend with him.

I remember that affair going on longer than a weekend. I think there was some correspondence and that he was back in touch with her months later when he returned to Paris.

A French rock star called Johnny Hallyday came a few times and drank heavily at the bar and during the meal with his friends he got drunker, and later passed out in the WC. I had to help him out to the saloon doors and into the waiting limo. He wasn't aggressive in the least. He kept saying to his entourage '*gotta give this guy here a big tip*'. Another rock star, Claude François, was a control freak, critical of the waitresses and the service, and he insisted on ordering for everybody at his table. This star probably thought that because he was paying for the meal, he could tell them what to eat. He left a teeny-weeny tip for the waitresses.

I would like to say he left a *'merci'* in his search for the toilet. But I suspect that would not be true.

Not a nice fellow.

The contrast in *politesse* between these 'stars' was probably no different than the contrasts in temperament of our other customers, more generally.

Many well-known jazz musicians came to see Leroy. I can't remember a single jazzman who threw his weight around or was rude, impatient, or nasty.

Nor me. My best memory of a musician luminary at that time is of Memphis Slim. He came to the restaurant quite a few times. More than any of the other stars. He felt like a 'regular'. I'm not sure whom he liked more. Leroy or the food. He enjoyed both a lot. He was a tall man and was always in a great mood. Nothing got under his skin. At least, nothing we did. He was one of the good guys. I remember he took an interest in all of us. And it seemed genuine. It was a good night when Memphis Slim dropped by,

Yes, it was.

There are two French stars whom I especially remember. Isabel Adjani and Maria Schneider. Isabel, because she came in more than a few times, and because she was so beautiful. She was still a few years younger than me, and I think she had just been nominated for an Oscar. So, she was a bona fide star. At that time, she was also being applauded (by me certainly) for her role in Polanski's film *The Tenant* which had just been released. It is still a favorite of mine. It is about a young man renting a small Parisian flat 4 or 5 floors up with a gorgeous girlfriend. Easy for a dishwasher in a 5th floor *chambre de bonne* to appreciate; even if Polanski's character goes mad and jumps out of his apartment window—twice! Hard to forget. Then the actress shows up at *Chez Haynes,* always with a flamboyant and jovial entourage—also difficult to forget. I was still the dishwasher then. I sometimes brushed past Isabel at her most beautiful on my way to the bar—not even your on-going diatribe about life and death and poverty could burst that balloon.

Really? My profound philosophical rants weren't more interesting? You have to be kidding.

My brush with Maria was altogether different. I was working as the barman by then. It was late in the evening, maybe midnight. There were not that many customers left, lots of empty tables. And this young woman walks in alone, not dressed up at all, jeans, no makeup. She was young, again about my age, and attractive. She didn't want a table. She just wanted to sit at the bar. I served her a drink. And made some small talk. Unlike you, my friend, I didn't make a habit of overtly hitting on single women at the bar, but I was happy to chat. She was less forthcoming. Quiet. I didn't recognize her at all. When I went to get some ice, one of the waitresses told me that she was Maria Schneider. Yes, that Maria Schneider. Very famous at the time. Her reputation for *Last Tango in Paris* was still relatively fresh. She looked and acted nothing like the character she portrayed in the film, and certainly not like the 'sex symbol' from the questionable scene with Marlon Brando. When I returned to the bar we continued to talk. I asked her what she did. She just said 'cinema'. I didn't want to look like I was another crazy fan, so I responded as if she was an usher in a local cinema and I asked her which one. She was happy enough to tell me she was an actress, but not in any boasting way. I talked about my writing and theatre. Not in any boasting way either—although in my case there was very little to boast about. At some point we sat down at an empty table and continued talking for about half an hour or so. My memory says she was quiet and somewhat troubled but was content enough to spend some time away from whatever was haunting her.

In the late-night shadow of *Chez Haynes*, Adjani and Schneider were a real study in contrasts. As for the WC, neither passed by me to use it on those nights. But I like to think that if they had, they both would have responded with a genuine '*merci*'.

15.

The Spanish Dwarf and Other Irregulars

THERE WERE A FEW MEMORABLE lesser-known regulars too.

The 'irregulars.' Regulars to the bar but 'irregular' in other ways. Like Odele who took Tex's tee shirt from the cloakroom one night, put it on, and pranced around the restaurant in it. When Tex—whom I had nick-named on his first day as a dishwasher because he was from Texas—demanded it back, she stripped it off, baring all, and dangled it in his face. Inexplicably, she was later hired as a waitress for a few months.

The Spanish dwarf comes to my mind. I know that today you're supposed to say short person.

That does sound better. After all, we are all irregular, but some people are treated more 'irregular' than others.

Leroy knew I spoke Spanish and told me to treat the short guy well. I never knew how Leroy had met Juanito in the first place. I would hoist Juanito up onto the barstool where he sat with his feet dangling about two feet from the floor. I told him there were some famous dwarfs in Velazquez's paintings, but Juanito couldn't care less, all the little man did was ogle the waitresses. He was as horny as a snake. After about five scotches he got weepy and made nasty cracks in heavily accented French at the waitresses. Finally, Leroy would come out and say, 'Okay Rafael, my man, time to get Juanito out of here'. And I would plead in Spanish with Juanito, but he wouldn't budge. 'Look', I'd say, 'I'm going to have to pick you up and take you out physically.' 'Oh yeah? You just try buster!' And I would come out from behind the bar and lift him up off the barstool, kicking and shouting. I'd say, 'I'm sorry, I really am, but this is what Leroy wants.' Juanito then called me *an hijo de puta*, a son of a whore, and a *cabrón*, which, as I said before, translates as Billy goat. I would put Juanito down on the sidewalk at the corner of Rue des Martyrs. 'Don't come back tonight, *hombre*, because you'll have to deal with Leroy.'

Then there was John, well-spoken and kind. A gentleman. Over the course of about six months, he came in regularly and would take his meal at the bar. He always came in alone. I think he enjoyed the opportunity to take in the American food and atmosphere and talk with other English-speaking expats. We soon got to know him well enough, although clearly not everything. And he asked more questions than he answered. I had been living in Paris for about 3 years by then and the little he did say about what he was doing in Paris never added up. Leroy didn't know him, and he didn't seem to have many connections to anyone or anything else. We joked about him being in the CIA, but we said that in passing. He was happy to talk about the theatre and art and projects we were all into and he bought a copy of my poems, so he was cool. Then he was gone. Didn't show up at the bar anymore. It turned out he was CIA. When he left Paris, he went to Iran. It wasn't long after that the Iranian Islamic revolution happened with heavy coverage in the press. The American Embassy in Tehran was overrun, and all the staff taken hostage. A few weeks later, someone came into the restaurant with a copy of the *International Herald Tribune*, and there was John in the photo, being released. He was one of a small group of people freed early because he was African American. Along with the women, the Iranians let him go because American blacks, they claimed, were victims of American oppression just like Iranians. The logic was impeccable.

There was also the director and a couple of the crew from the Carolyn Carlson Dance Research Group at the Paris Opera. They came in, maybe a dozen times. She maybe once, just to eat. The others generally dropped by for drinks after a show. I quizzed them about the work and what they were doing. Told them about our work. They invited me to my first dance opera. Told me to be early. It turned out to be a seven-hour show. I had never been to the opera before. Nor had I ever attended a ballet, contemporary or not. I sat with them in the lighting booth. Great seats, but seven hours? I was not sure I could handle that. My first thought was how to get out during one of the breaks. It turned out to be a non-problem. I was completely blown away by the show. The sheer scale was astounding. Very different from the intimate pieces by Beckett, Ionesco and Pinter which had been my main influence. I followed up with trips to Pina Bausch's Wuppertal Theatre at the Theatre de la Ville. And Robert Wilson's *Einstein on the Beach* with Philip Glass's music. Very eye-opening stuff at the time.

And there was Namio too, a wealthy Japanese car salesman who also painted. He always treated us to champagne. He drank horrific amounts of scotch, and wine too. At closing time, I would call him a cab and gently slide him into it. One evening he told us how, as a young man, he had volunteered as a kamikaze pilot. It was a great honor for his family, he said. The day he was supposed to fly his suicide mission, the war ended, and he was grounded. It was terrible, Namio told us, so shameful for him and his family. In his anger and sadness and frustration, he stole a rowboat in Yokohama harbor and started rowing east, toward the US to exact his own revenge. He was pretty far out at sea when he was picked up by a US destroyer. The captain couldn't get a word out of Namio, so the battleship kept going to San Francisco where Namio disappeared. There, he made his way into the burgeoning Beatnik scene around Ferlinghetti's City Lights bookstore. Namio went to art school and miraculously became legal. His family must have hoped he had died at sea. They were surprised when they found out he was alive. He begged them to allow him to come home, and his family said okay, but for a short stay only. Namio couldn't stay in Japan even if he was sort of a hero now to his family. His family relations got him a well-paid job in Paris, selling Japanese cars. All he had to do was take visiting Japanese car industry bigshots around Paris to visit nightclubs and whorehouses. He could hold his liquor well, but once in a rare while he'd kind of break down. The stern Japanese reserve would crack, and Namio would quietly say this is what Japanese patriotism gets you. 'I know what I am, I'm not a painter, I'm a glorified man-Friday with a bit of the pimp thrown in.'

It wasn't obvious when I first met Namio that he was doing battle with his own personal history quite so fiercely. It should have been more obvious: he was an older guy with money, living alone, still partying like an undergrad in residence. But what did I know? I had just arrived in Paris: a younger guy with no history to speak of, other than a handful of philosophy courses and a crumbling two-year relationship that would fully and mercifully die a few months later. It hardly compares to the unfathomable shame of failing to exit one's life in a mass suicide attack from the sky. I assumed Namio was a successful painter, which was so cool, although I cannot remember what his paintings looked like. I recall he was a generous man with an amazing apartment in a fashionable part of Paris. I have memories of a couple of amazing parties at his place. Indeed, it was through one of these parties that I was given the two most important household items of my time in Paris. I had just moved out of the hotel on *Rue Saint-André des Arts* into my two rooms. The rooms were mainly furnished except there was no decent bed. After a few nights the couch was getting uncomfortable. One of the guests at the party said she was throwing out some things, including a bed and a typewriter. A typewriter? It was not electric, but, nevertheless, a working typewriter! I'd only brought pen and pencils on the airplane. A couple of days later, Harry, his cousin and I went to her flat to pick up the items. It was on the other side of Paris. I only needed a mattress and the typewriter, but she insisted we take the box spring as well. We didn't have a car or money for a taxi, so we threw ourselves on the mercy of Parisian public transportation. As Harry later told me; 'We moved them from one side of Paris to the other by bus, all very much to the disgust of the other riders.' I remember avoiding the stares and looks by just gazing out the window at the magnificent city which had just become my new home, hoping this awkward piece of impromptu street theatre would quickly pass.

16.

Encounters with Authority

Few, if any of the staff at Chez Haynes, were legally in France, or had anything resembling long term visas. Our illegality hovered in the background of our lives, like an impending storm, but nothing ever happened. The tempest never burst.

I never carried my passport with me or any other formal I.D. When I was stopped—and the cops (*les flics*) commonly in a group of about ten or more did stop me—my *carte orange* would suffice. At first their sheer numbers were a little intimidating, but they were polite and reasonable. For the most part they ignored me. No matter where or when I was riding or sauntering through the city. Late night was the same as early morning. I never felt fearful of them; or of any of the other kinds of authorities in Paris. Metro gendarmes, tax collectors, bank officials, municipal bureaucrats, even the street sweepers. I essentially sidestepped whatever sensors of disorder might have provoked them. And very quickly the city became home. Inside the *peripherique*. The suburbs, or *banlieue,* felt a bit different. But then I am sure that was the case for most Parisians as well.

Paris was quite manageable as cities go. And not just because of *la carte orange*. It was also a fantastic walking city. After work, if I missed the last metro, I would walk back home at 2 or 3 in the morning—from the 9th *arrondissement* near the top of Paris to the 14th *arrondissement* near the bottom. Only about 5 miles depending on the route. It was always quiet as I started down Rue des Martyrs. Then I had a choice. At first, I took the most direct route which was Boulevard du Faubourg Montmartre. It sliced down southeast towards the river, lost its 'Faubourg' designation on the way down, and ended at Les Halles or what was left of it. In those days, it was not much more than a large hole in the ground and then a construction site. It went on forever. In space and time. I don't remember the walk being very interesting in the middle of the night. Nothing much happening other than some amazing Parisian Boulevard architecture quietly sleeping as I slipped by. It was picturesque but after a few years I began to simply take it for granted. As eventually I did Paris. Except for random moments when I suddenly became conscious of where I was and was immediately blown away. Paris, France! Too easy to overlook when day to day life intervenes. As it always does. On other nights I would turn east along the Grands Boulevards then turn south on Rue Saint Denis. Which is where my walk got more interesting. Saint Denis was very active at that time of night, awake with ranks of prostitutes and hawkers and bars and cafes.

Near the Gare de L'Est, off Saint Denis was the Rue Sainte Apolline, also a hangout for prostitutes. And there was a wonderful paintbrush store in that street, an amazing place. I've forgotten the name of the shop, but it was like Ali Baba's cave for paintbrushes. There was a whole section for sign painting brushes, and another for brushes for movie billboards. There were some cinemas then near Barbès where they still painted billboards for films that were showing, especially films from Egypt and Algeria. Every time I left the store one of the prostitutes would wink at me and say, 'hey lover boy, you wanna see my brush?'

I remember lots of colored lights happening. Lots of activity. There might even have been a typewriter store. At 3 a.m. in the morning, I never stopped for an in-depth investigation of the area. Although I usually slowed down for a better look around as I made my way down to the Place du Chatelet, the Seine and Pont au Change. It was normally silent crossing the l'Île de Cité unless the bells of Notre Dame, a block over, pealed two or three late-night bells. Then it was onto the trinity of St. Michels—over Pont St. Michel, across Quai St. Michel and up Boulevard St. Michel, past Le Jardin de Luxembourg which Tex and I sometimes jogged in. He was an excellent soccer player, even practiced at the first division Paris St. Germain F.C. during his time in Paris.

My route then continued along to Port Royale, past the *Obervatoire*, onto Avenue Denfert Rochereau, down to Place Denfert Rochereau and the Catacombs. Everywhere, more museums and gorgeous buildings of note. Finally, I crossed Boulevard Montparnasse and entered my local district, the 14th *arrondissement*. Then it was down Avenue General Leclerc to Place d'Alésia (my metro stop) where a quick 5-minute jaunt down Avenue Jean Moulin—hero of the Resistance—took me home. To Square de Chatillon, a hidden little residential cobblestone courtyard with a small hotel. I was in number seven.

Paris *intra muros* is a small city compared to New York or London. You can walk across it in a few hours. You used to say that in New York they built taller buildings and it expanded upward, in London they built houses side by side, and it expanded outwards, but in Paris they divided the existing living space in two or three and it remained the same. New York taller, London fatter, Paris suck in your belly.

Paris always looked beautifully preserved, even as renovations regenerated the city from within. Certainly, that was the way it appeared in the middle of the night as I journeyed home. Except for the Tour Montparnasse which was a recent eye sore. I usually walked back on my own, but I remember doing the full walk back from *Chez Haynes* with Vince––a tall good-natured guy from Lynchburg, Virginia. I remember his hometown because the name always sounded ominous to me. He and I had survived a very lean period during the heatwave of 1976 on the calories from many liter bottles of Ober Pils Bière which cost less than 2 francs each at the time. He could be even crazier than we were on our worst nights. On this night, he and I drank at more than a few bars all the way back. By the time we got to Boulevard St Michel we were well past the limit of rational behavior. I vaguely remember we got into some reckless mischief with car mirrors along the street. Mischief is a nice way to describe kicking off a half dozen side view mirrors from a Mercedes or Porsche just for the amazing feel and sound of the crack as it came away from the car. Revenge theatre? Theatre Noir? Or just plain theatre of the vandal? No excuse. When we reached my building, Vince pulled out a broken side mirror he had picked up from the street, He was claiming it as a souvenir. I saw it as damning evidence of criminal behavior. I grabbed it from him, staggered into the bin room and stuffed it down through as many bags of garbage as I could, up to my shoulder, hoping it would not be found. If it had been found, I knew the foreign kid at the top would be *le premier suspect*. Fortunately, it was never discovered.

You don't want to be a suspect. Once you're in the clutches of the French bureaucracy, you're in for life. But I wanted to be legal--sort of. I had twice stood in line at six in the morning outside the Préfecture de Police on the Île de la Cité. I had gathered the necessary documents. The line was a long one, it started outside, and continued down the block toward Notre Dame. We shuffled along slowly. The crowd consisted of poor foreigners. The rich foreigners hired lawyers and avoided the queue. I would finally reach the building entrance at first light. The queue inched up the three-hundred-year-old stone stairs, up to the third floor. I remember babies crying. The steps worn shiny by the millions of shoes that had trodden there before me, and shoes is probably saying a lot. The poor people wore everything but leather shoes, more likely wooden clogs, rubber sandals, galoshes, espadrilles. At last, I stood in front of the guichet window where a stern-looking woman, lips painted *à la* Édith Piaf, was smoking a cigarette. I pushed my sheaf of documents below the guichet window. I didn't dare smile. I tried to look neutral. The woman shuffled through my papers, looked up at me and said, with the cigarette still hanging from her lips, 'there are some documents missing'. She rattled off a jumble of numbers and letters: 44A, 72C, and 89B. 'Come back in a week.' I started to ask what was missing, but she said, 'come on, come on, *allez, allez, je n'ai pas toute la journée pour vous, moi.* I haven't got time for you people.' She raised her chin and said in a loud voice: *'Next! Au suivant!'* I turned away and saw the next supplicant, an Arab woman, her head covered, a baby in her arms. I couldn't help thinking of Stefan Zweig's book "*Fouché*", about the fellow who toppled Robespierre and became the police chief, who invented the institution of the concierges, during the revolution; a spy in every building, and hence the name for the old prison of La Conciergerie.

I found the less identification I produced, the better. I was fortunate. Clearly western looking, even French, at a quick glance if I tied my scarf correctly. Not a member of any group or stereotype the people in charge were concerned with—other than, *peut-être*, being a little too young to completely trust. Even when I fell ill and spent a week in the hospital because my heart suddenly opted for a change in rhythm, I simply gave them my passport and claimed to have no health insurance. I might have had some student coverage in Canada, but I remembered Darian describing his experience when he went to hospital in Montpellier for a malaria episode which he had contracted in Africa. He was a Canadian doing a doctoral degree in Bordeaux. He gave them his Canadian Health Insurance details and from then on it was a nightmare trying to connect the two systems. In the end they extracted something out of the Canadian system, but he ended up having to pay a hefty chunk himself. I simply threw myself on the mercy of the system. They asked me if I lived in Paris. I said yes. They asked me if I had anything more than *carte orange* to prove I did. I said no. They asked me if I had any insurance. I said no. They asked me if I had any money or assets. I said no. They covered me, and from then on, in their wisdom or through sheer tedium, the authorities left me alone. Almost.

One time at your place, five floors up, you gave a small party, and the neighbors complained about the loud music. The young gendarmes showed up around midnight. They had lumbered up the last two floors. The door to your apartment was open, and there they were, two cops out of breath trying to get our attention as people filed in and out, and others smoked in the hallway. The police told us we were making too much noise, and we turned down the music and offered them a glass of wine. They started talking to us; well, to the girls more than to the boys. Some of us were standing near the Turkish toilet in the hall. The cops stayed for about an hour, took a few leaks in the squat job, and thanked us for the wine, which they said was very good. Damn right, it was good. Leroy had given us some top-quality stuff.

I remember when they first arrived, I apologized and said I had not caused a problem before. They said the complaint was not the first one they had received. It was just the first time they had come to my door. I tried a joke about the climb up the stairs being a bit much for them. It didn't go well. They started writing me out a ticket. I said *'doucement, s'il vous plaît. Je suis un poète.'*. It turned out to be a warning ticket. A full written out ticket with the amount 'zero francs' circled. I was so grateful. I have always thought what a great idea. Start soft. It worked. I was much quieter from then on.

You should have framed the *amende.*

I should have. I may have it buried in a box somewhere. I did get to know the old lady who had reported me. She lived beneath me and turned out to be very amenable and open-minded. And was very patient. I assumed she would hate me, a young foreigner up above making noise, doing young-guy-outsider type things. Like having parties. But she was wonderful. She invited me in a couple of times, and we talked. She was in her 80s back then, from a different century. She lived alone but said she was used to it. We talked about her history in Square de Chatillon. She told me she had lived there for a long time. When she was young, her husband was captured by the Germans in the First World War and spent a few years in Germany as a prisoner of war; then her son was captured in the Second World War and endured the same fate. Both survived, but they were no longer alive when I spoke to her. She didn't begrudge the Germans any longer. I am not sure I would have been so obliging.

I asked her about the bullet holes in the walls of some of the buildings in our little square. She told me that happened when Paris was being liberated. We lived in the southern part of Paris and the liberation troops came up through Porte d'Orléans. We were on the northern part of the square and the Germans had occupied our rooms firing across at the hotel where the French liberation soldiers were. The evidence was still there thirty years later. At least on our side. Liberation holes. When I stuck my head out my French windows, I could see holes on the walls, around the windows. I assume some bullets came through the window as well, but that damage had been repaired. She had lived through all that mayhem. When the shooting started, she would go down with other neighbors into the basement. And wait for the all-clear.

I suppose it is hard to imagine that urban atmosphere today. I've seen too many movies about that era. I confuse what I really imagine and what I am unconsciously borrowing or imagining second-hand from films I've seen.

Even back then, those war years were decades distant. Certainly not part of any memory I shared. But it was fascinating to see some of its more poignant remnants on the walls and to hear her voice recalling memories of her story during that time.

Life in our Paris may have been uncomfortable with few indoor toilets and fewer phones, but life was more relaxed than today, communication was slower, and the police seemed more tolerant. Maybe that was because the May riots of 1968 were still fresh in the collective memory of Paris.

No authority wanted to see those events again, any time soon.

And we were so oblivious of our own age too. I remember one Sunday evening, five or six of us went to *La Coupole* for dinner. In those days you could still go there without a reservation. The restaurant had a mythic quality for me because I knew that the great Alberto Giacometti, painter, and sculptor, used to go there with friends, always after midnight, and while he ate, he drew on the table paper. Sometimes his friends tore off a piece with a drawing or two, but other times the waiters threw out the table papers along with the drawings. And did you know that he and Beckett were friends?

Not until you told me. Beckett's work I knew and liked. You put me onto Giacometti and his fabulous walking sculptures. The fact that they were friends was icing on some kind of proverbial cake.

When a client was wanted on the phone at La Coupole, a waiter walked through the restaurant holding up a blackboard with the client's name written on it in chalk, and at the same time the waiter shouted out the name of the client. When we put on your play, *Black to Black*, at the American Centre we used that as free publicity. A few times a night we'd phone La Coupole asking for Monsieur Light, and the waiter would walk around with LIGHT written on the blackboard and shouting out *Monsieur Light, Monsieur Light.*

I am not sure we drummed up much business. The La Coupole clientele of the time was not our natural audience.

The evening in question we were celebrating someone's birthday. Next to our table was an American couple, not more than sixty years old. I turned to them and said, well, how does it feel being old? The woman turned to us and said 'it feels awful, so enjoy yourselves'. We all laughed. I felt ashamed of myself.

But we did follow her advice. We enjoyed ourselves.

17.

Driving Backwards in Paris

IF OUR ENCOUNTERS WITH AUTHORITY were generally blessed, there were times when the absence of authority was just plain lucky. Especially when substances were involved.

We were young, our bodies could take it, the wine, the beer, the cocaine, the weed, the poppers (isoamyl nitrate). Looking back, it was pretty insane, and yet our creativity, our *rage de vivre* continued undiminished. Yeah, I know we have to mention sex at *Chez Haynes*, and yes, there was quite a lot of it; some would call it fast and loose, others warm and sentimental, generous and exhilarating, faithful and jealous. There were broken hearts and tears too. And we drank too much probably, we let go and laughed our heads off, and there were times of leaden love-sadness.

That rings true to me. During these most impulsive years, before growing older came along, we essentially glided through an era of sexual inconsequence. Nothing catastrophic happened to defy our youthful defiance. The sexual revolution and the pill were history. The fear of pregnancy was already a decade in the past. The fear of AIDS was a decade in the future and antibiotic resistant bacteria was still science fiction. The culture of alcohol was synonymous with the good life—public health meekly suggesting we limit our consumption to a different level of alcoholism. Drink was the great overture of the day.

The staff could drink as much as they wanted, as long as they didn't wobble too much on their feet when they served the clients. Yes, we all drank, and on busy nights, as the hours dragged on, the waitresses, bless them all, kept going with tequila sunrises and whisky sours. Don would come out of the kitchen and order a Jack Daniels, Blackjack as he called it. And as I already mentioned, there was cocaine, too, once in a while. Great stuff, made you fast like a dancer, daring, self-confident. And Leroy was generous. One Monday evening Leroy gave everyone on the staff a bottle of Mouton Rothschild. He had won big at the Longchamp racetrack and was feeling even more generous than usual. Around that time my grandmother died and left me a thousand dollars; and I bought the second-hand VW. It was a change in my life. A big change. No more carte orange, remember? And parking was no problem in those days in Paris. Nobody ever paid their parking tickets.

The one time I remember driving in Paris, I got tangled up in the giant roundabout circling the Arc de Triomphe on Place Charles de Gaulle. Eight lanes at a minimum, but back then there were no lane markings to indicate one from the other. I entered, got forced toward the center and circled around and around for half an hour before I could find my way out the other side. Never again. And I swear I was substance free.

Sometimes we mixed our substances. My uncle worked at the Iranian embassy in Paris. Every so often he'd give me a two-kilo tin of Persian caviar. One evening we found ourselves in my one-room apartment with some of the *Chez Haynes* staff.

183 Rue Saint Martin. I still have good memories of that street and that room. And many, many more that lost their way on route to my consciousness.

The conversations at such gatherings were always interesting, unexpected, staccato. The topics ranged far and wide, and with a little help from the wine and the weed we touched upon films, photography, dance, theatre, painting, and more. My place was small, maybe ten square meters, and we sat on the floor and on the mattress. We also brought two bottles of vodka and a few lemons from *Chez Haynes*. I opened the tin of caviar and with a soup spoon scooped out some of that black goo, squeezed lemon juice on it, took a swig of the vodka and then a 'toke' from the joint. I passed the caviar tin and the spoon to one of the girls. And it went around. Then somebody had the bright idea to hand out some poppers, which as you may remember makes your heart rate jump to 200 beats a minute--for a few minutes, like the Apollo rocket right there in your chest. And out of the blue, your cousin who was also there took a popper and a few seconds later announced she suffered from a heart condition. Panic stations! I suggested she drink a glass of water, which she did. The rush passed in a few seconds and your cousin and the rest of us were relieved, and that's putting it very mildly, that she hadn't died.

Memories of that evening have returned! Thank you. Mainly, I think, because of the caviar. And the poppers. And the heart episode. But, for the life of me I cannot think of which of my cousins might have been there. Maybe Harry's cousin. She seemed to attract unwanted events. Bentley was also there. All of us devouring our way through spoonful after spoonful of this delicious and expensive egg dish that would have cost a fortune in the best Parisian restaurants.

And one night, a few weeks later, after closing at *Chez Haynes,* I drove you and Laura and Scott back to their apartment on Réaumur where we smoked a joint and proceeded to get very drunk. I have forgotten if we had a reason to get soused, probably not.

It was that night I remember as the 'tequila night'. We went to Laura and her boyfriend Scott's apartment. They were near the end of their relationship, and I remember him being a little morose that night. He didn't join in. In retrospect maybe that was a good idea. I don't remember drinking anything but tequila, and smoking lots of weed. Again, we brought the bottle from *Chez Haynes*. Leroy was secretly killing us with his generosity.

The point is that at three or four in the morning we decided to call it a night. I wanted to drive you home all the way to the Porte d'Orléans. But I knew damn well there was no way I could drive across Paris, from the second *arrondissement* to your place. I pulled out of the parking space on Réaumur, and for some reason, I began to drive backward the wrong way down Reaumur, a one-way street. It must have been a good three hundred meters, right on past Sebastopol. I remember backing up by looking in the side mirrors. A miracle we didn't die, and another miracle was that there were no cops around and very few cars.

After that slick backward driving move, I have a strong and distinct memory of us driving forward along the Rue de Rivoli, its arches in the mist and rain and lights sliding by, and you suddenly shouting out 'look, I'm driving. I'm driving,' with this amazed look on your face. Like, you were watching from afar and just became aware of this marvelous feat of muscle memory. ('Look, no hands.') Which I guess it was. Until that moment, not for a second had I thought our late-night journey was out of the ordinary. Then I began to wonder. What the hell are we doing? Somehow you parked. Thankfully, driving is mostly an unconscious activity; and your brain decided not to let your mind intervene.

You passed out on the floor of the apartment, and I fell asleep on the bed.

On a floor you 'pass out'. On a bed you 'fall asleep'. The outcome was the same: oblivion by alcohol.

At eight in the morning, the phone rang, and I answered it saying in as cheery a voice as I could muster, '*Chez Haynes Restaurant, bonsoir, how can I help you?*'

You may have thought you were cheery and pitch perfect, but it was force of habit that got you through the greeting. I don't know who was on the other end and I was in no condition to care, but once habit deserted you, it took you some time to figure out where you were, who you were and what planet the caller was from.

All this happened a long time ago, and we could handle the drinking.

Really? Could we?

Thinking back, I admit we were quite often drunk, and the odd thing is I can't remember the hangovers. Now at 75 I have an occasional drink, say every six months, or so, and never get really drunk, but now the morning hangovers are tremendous, like Mack semis careening around in my skull. Just awful. Takes me a day to recuperate. How did we do it? We weren't doing any exercise; we weren't physically especially fit. And yet I never had a hangover in the *Chez Haynes* days.

The hangovers were there. We were just able to shake them off more easily. They did not wreck the next day as they do now. And they did not stop us from doing the same thing again the next night. I do remember learning to drink a lot of water and taking two aspirins before falling asleep. It worked well when I remembered to do it. It rarely (meaning never) worked (meaning happened) just before 'passing out' on a floor.

At the time I did not notice how many adults around me were heavy drinkers. That was because I never hung out with adults, especially in the evenings. Was I an adult? Yes and no. More no than yes.

I don't think pleading we were not adults at the time will justify the stupidity to which these memories confess. Even relying on youth as an excuse is a stretch. However, it was a place and time when the epitome of public health was limiting alcohol consumption to one bottle of wine a day. If we sometimes exchanged that wine for tequila, surely, we were still within the Parisian bounds of 'almost acceptable'.

I knew that Leroy was a total alcoholic because I counted the bottles he drank from the bar. I kept drinking until I was in my late fifties. Did I become an alcoholic? Probably. I was drinking two bottles of wine by myself as soon as I got home from work in the evening. This of course was many years after *Chez Haynes*. I looked forward to it, the drink, I mean. I always remembered how much wine there was in the icebox, and if there was less than a full bottle, I would make sure to buy some on the way home, even if it meant going all the way to Nation where there was an *alimentation générale* open late. Did I look forward to that first drink? Of course, you have no idea.

I think I have an idea. But maybe just an idea. Paris was the apex of my drinking. Not that I refrained from over-indulgence later on, just terminated its perpetual motion.

After the first gulp I'd wait for the knock-knock, 'hello I'm here'. But the first gulp was never enough. I needed two or three to feel that first buzz which told me everything was all right. With scotch it was easier, the knock-knock came faster, one gulp usually got me started. And no, I didn't give a shit if the scotch or the wine was good or bad, all I cared about was the alcohol content. How can you not drink once you've known that warm, beautiful feeling telling you you're all right with the world? I have an iron will, and I finally stopped hitting the sauce. I have an iron will because as the biologist Dawkins says, I won the genetic lottery. I didn't will my iron will. You don't will to be lazy or dyslexic or have a flawed digestive system or smelly feet or a sense of humor.

I think we are on the edge of our decades long debate about free will here. In saying you didn't will your iron will, I assume you are saying self-discipline is just genetics. Is youthful stupidity just genetics? Do we have an excuse after all? Even though I continued to work in bars in London for several more years, I too curtailed the heavy drinking. I attribute it to age and chance in partner and circumstance as much as any genetic mutation. But maybe that's splitting hairs.

I still miss alcohol today, fifteen years later. I quit in 2006. And when I am invited out to dinner, it is still difficult not to drink. I sometimes fall off the wagon. I see now that most parties are just an excuse for getting soused with friends. I stopped smoking when I stopped the booze. I don't miss smoking. I used to love smoking and drinking when I did the International Herald Tribune crossword puzzle. I stopped doing the crossword puzzle. Stopped the weed too when I had children. This has been a bit of a digression, but we said we'd keep this dialogue about those years honest, open, even if it means being a little gushy at moments.

Gushy works. Honesty is sometimes a little more troubling. At some point near the end of my stay in Paris, I think the drinking may have caught up with me. I was only 29. I don't know if you remember but I came down with a wicked case of tonsillitis. I knew the symptoms well, as I had been prone to it as a kid, and it became a regular visitor. Fortunately, antibiotics always worked brilliantly. I remember Laura suggesting a local GP near the Place d'Alésia. A young doctor, just setting up his practice. I told him that I just needed antibiotics, but he insisted on a full work up including an ECG. I am pretty sure I was very close to being his first client, certainly his first ECG patient. He pulled out the machine, still gleaming and wrapped in plastic. It was all cords and plugs and sensors which he appeared to fumble with. It didn't help that he looked like Woody Allen at his most ungainly. A half hour into hooking up the machine and sticking and unsticking nodes to my chest, I thought he was going to electrocute me. He finally got it set up and the reading began ticking out. Then he started to look alarmed. Then I started to look alarmed. My heartbeat was all over the place although I did not feel anything different. That's when he referred me to St. Joseph's hospital. It was very close, maybe a ten-minute walk at most, but he insisted I take a taxi. Which scared me.

A taxi, eh? Spending big time for the ticker is understandable.

I pictured myself dropping dead on the sidewalk, which may have been what he pictured as well. I was immediately admitted and hooked up with all kinds of tests which delayed any antibiotics. For the first few days I felt increasingly ill. When you and the *Chez Haynes* people came by to see me, the look of sympathetic dread on your faces was not comforting. A week later, I was released. After finally getting some antibiotics, I was feeling great, but my heartbeat was still lop-sided. It was diagnosed as lone atrial fibrillation, for which the treatment was rat poison. Warfarin. And a second drug, the side effect of which meant keeping fully out of the sun. When I asked them what caused it, they were unsure—hence the 'lone' designation. They said it could have been something to do with the tonsillitis—I knew the irregularity was not there a week earlier because I performed *Black to Black* at the American Center on Boulevard Raspail and, to help me focus in the wings before I went on, I would close my eyes and count my pulse.

I never knew you even focused like this. Is that what you always did before you went on stage?

Yes, that was my way of relieving my nerves—mainly for my one-man shows. Anyway, the cardiologist added nonchalantly as I was dressing to leave, that the condition could be due to heavy drinking. That might bring it on. He was not sure. I was not happy. I had, after all, been rigorously following their public health guidelines and drinking a bottle of wine a day. I still have the condition over forty years later. Day after day. it continues to relentlessly pound out its random beat. I am still unaware of it, but I am now on a cocktail of older-man substances to give my heart a fighting chance. So far so good. I never fully stopped drinking, but I did become a little more health conscious—maybe that was a parting gift from Paris. There, a little extra gushy for you.

Anyway, we can always edit out. That was also one of the rules of this dialogue.

We haven't edited out anything yet. But we have not remembered everything yet either.

As parting gifts go, it's pretty bad, worse than the proverbial gold watch from GM, that's General Motors. I had worked the night shift for four months at the GM plant in Flint, Michigan, before I graduated from art school in 1968. Absolutely brutal. But not as bad as your heart going wonky on you.

You were a UAW man, also? So was I. For three months. I worked the night shift in a Chrysler factory the summer before I left for Paris. So, are we just union guys at heart?

I've forgotten whether I was union or not. But I do remember the atmosphere was tense. My stint at GM was in 1968. America was polarized. The Vietnam War, the civil rights movement. Some of the workers packed guns at work on the assembly line. Others were stoned all the time. The job paid well. But back to your heart. It makes sense in a French way; the Parisian culture vultures always favor the artistic and creative dead.

I know you are talking about my death by heart attack. But I am not sure what to make of that?

Okay. I won't go on a rant here against the critics, the self-appointed midwives of culture. Critics of all stripes.

I am sure critics have no interest in my heart. Beating or not.

While I'm on the subject of this dialogue, let me say that I don't believe in the soul.

That's harsh. Some critics have souls. What do the young say today. Laugh out loud?

Selling our souls in Paris. That would have been a good title for this book.

I am not so keen. In the first place, it's a hard sell if it doesn't exist. And secondly, what else would the soul exist for if not to be sold. Every time we open our mouths, put brush to canvas, pen to paper, even a smile or a wink across a crowded restaurant, we are selling our souls.

Most people come to Paris to find themselves. We often lost ourselves and it was fine. And what you say about selling one's soul sounds right.

Thanks. Maybe it's just the word for me.

My version of the soul has to do with the dreams and hopes that I was carrying around. Selling them was good, it made room for more dreams and hopes, unclogging the metaphysical plumbing.

Thank you for not saying 'religious' plumbing. I can just about accept the idea that selling one's soul is little more than aesthetic foible and compromise, and on occasion, willing submission to one or more of the seven sins. But I am happy to accept your connection to dreams.

Leroy hired dreamers, artists, poets, writers.

Leroy. Now, there was an amazing soul.

18.

The Almost Bearable Lightness of Being

ALONGSIDE *CHEZ HAYNES*, IN ADDITION to books and stories, there was much getting out of our minds too, with sundry drugs.

As we just described in some detail. It sounds like you are suggesting a second installment.

Why not?

It will undoubtedly take us somewhere totally different.

Nothing like getting stoned, standing on the back platform of a bus going along the Seine, and lighting up a joint. Later these bus platforms were deemed too dangerous. What a loss. Bouncing along, careening to the left and right when the bus turned, and of course you could talk to the girls, somehow bouncing back and forth on that back platform made talking and flirting so natural. Bumping into a beautiful woman about to light up her Gauloise by the railing, and I'd whip out my Zippo. Remember those?

I didn't smoke but I remember Zippos and the Gauloise. Not as clearly as I remember the girls swishing by on the bus, though.

Next thing you know we hop off by the Rue Bonaparte, have a beer. And it turns out she's studying philosophy. In Spain you say the road from the dance floor to the bedroom is mighty long, well, from *un peu de philosophie* it's mighty short.

Especially in Paris. More so when facilitated with a joint. In retrospect weed facilitated that whole time more than we cared to admit. Dangled the secret of something before us. Insight? Folly? Both? I can't say our best work flowed from our late-night experiments with words and smoke. Many a morning spent pouring through nonsense looking for those *bon mots* that had us rolling over in laughter the night before. But I do think many of our best times flowed from that finely rolled miniature paper baguette. Man Ray should have painted it as well. Maybe he did? Blue, Red, Green, Rainbow? Would Pompidou, its skeleton, and innards all inside out, have accepted it?

There was whisky too. That was available, and it was legal. I told Leroy whenever I borrowed a bottle, only once in a while, from his stock in the *cave*.

But did you replace it?

Sure, I did.

He never replaced the booze on the mirrored shelf behind the bar. When he drank, we refilled the whisky bottles. It was the first task of the evening. But I interrupted you.

You know all this. Why not get it out in the open, here? It was not the case so much during the *Chez Haynes* years, but afterwards. And then it got worse. I suffered from depression for years. So, I drank. I told myself it was self-medication. Lame excuse, I know.

That was not you back then. But I know, later, for a while it became the worst of times.

About five years ago, the black dogs slinked away; I don't know why. My moods in those years were triggered by lack of money, a sense of failure in my life, but they were in the category of moods, teetering on depression. The fear of death is healthy I think; some philosophers claim that thinking about death every day is good for you, keeps the mind clear and lucid, but when the demons come in the night, well, it ain't that easy, and somehow reaching out to God doesn't help because I can't get myself to believe. I just can't pretend about that. But it's frightening. To paraphrase Brendan Behan, being a daylight atheist is easy, being a nighttime atheist, that's hard. So yes, I was used to getting a little down, like six feet under, beneath the asphalt, cavorting with the earthworms.

Can't get any lower than that, eh?

That's more than 'a little' down. We all got down. Sometimes far down. That came with the territory. Day to day existence, frustration, self-doubt. ('What am I fucking doing here?') The ambitions and delusions of youth. Right up there with sex, love and fame. We shared them all. But you did frequently take a step further. Added death to the mix. Although, I was never worried about you. Suicide was never a serious option. Not that I could see. But death certainly was a more visceral (fearful?) theme (preoccupation?) for you than the far-in-the-distance, philosophical concept it was for the rest of us. We were in our twenties. The end was not yet in our muscles and bones. Not viscerally anyway. But the idea was always present. It usually popped up in conversations alongside God and hell and the perils of not believing, laced with a soothing ration of wine. Or an unruly swig of whisky. Or a reckless gulp of tequila. We teased you about it—like the evening around the table in *Chez Haynes*. "One of us won't be here next year". But we were all there the next summer, and the next winter. And mostly, I think, we are all still here almost 50 years later. As, too, is death. But now with a little less patience and a broader grin. Almost a smirk.

Death's nag is chomping at the bit. In my small painting studio in the sixteenth *arrondissment* of all places, I had a bottle of Ballantine's on the shelf. That's middle-of-the-line blended scotch. I wasn't going to splurge on some expensive single malt stuff. All I cared about, as I said earlier, was the alcohol content which led to the buzz I was after. And you know I kept a gun, a revolver to be exact, next to the bottle.

Drugs, Drink and Death?

Why did I do it? Don't ask.

I did ask. Back then I asked.

In retrospect, it was braggadocio perhaps,

It was more interesting than that.

I had no bullets for the weapon, but it kept the lights on in my skull. Buying bullets illegally was easy at the flea market at Montreuil. My Iranian uncle lent me the *chambre de bonne* to use as a studio. It was small but big enough to paint in and perhaps shoot myself. Why is there a stigma about suicide? Some people say it's selfish and cruel to those loved ones left behind, and so on. Listen up, if you reach that stage, nobody loves you anymore, you're sure nobody loves you, you're just a note at the end of a shitty tune--why not?

I remember that first tiny art studio of yours well. It was a wonderful space. Hidden away along narrow corridors of countless attic rooms once reserved for the servants of the bourgeoisie. There was just enough wall and floor space to work and hang your paintings. With a large table or counter for paints and trays and brushes and a shelf left over for an empty bottle of Ballantine's and the gun. A Colt? A Smith and Wesson?

I have no idea. I've forgotten.

I'm afraid that's the limit of my knowledge of guns. I don't know if I told you but that was the space in my head when, years later, I wrote the catalogue for your UNESCO show. *The Outsider Paintings*? We had some great times with that gun and bottle of Ballantine's. There is a terrific photo of you and I and our surprised fellow artist friend Bentley, standing in the studio, huddled together for what must have been an early selfie. It captures his startled eyes when he suddenly realized you were holding a gun. Admittedly unloaded. But I am not sure he knew that.

I set up a darkroom there, remember?

I remember you beginning your experiments using your painting tools—brushes and spray cans and developer chemicals on canvasses and materials you had previously photosensitized—to reveal photographic images of themes you were exploring in your art. I was impressed by the originality of the process and the power of the result.

Oh, yes. I became a darkroom wizard. Bear with me here a moment. You must remember those were the days before digital photography. Taking and making photographs was complicated, and that's why most people took their roll of negative film to a shop that developed it, and then from the contact sheet, they chose the prints they wanted. Well, I learned to do all this myself. I converted the mansard room that my uncle had put at my disposal into a darkroom. I put in a red light, which was necessary when developing and printing black and white photographs. I bought an enlarger that projected the negative 35mm film frame onto a sheet of photographic paper for a certain length of time, usually about half a minute. Next, I dipped the exposed paper into a tray with developer liquid which brought out the positive image. When the photo had emerged to my satisfaction, I slipped it into the stopper bath a few minutes, which stopped the imaged from developing any further. Finally, the paper went into the fixer bath. And finally, I washed the print. All this was for only one photo. I'll spare you the details for larger and smaller prints, and for color photos. It was more complicated.

I was in that darkroom dozens of times. I helped on occasion. Or at least I thought I was helping. You may have just been humoring me. I do know you perfected it for many of our other projects as well as your own work.

I wanted to do large prints, a square meter and more. I discovered a photo-sensitive canvas sold in Germany in rolls one meter twenty wide and ten meters long, and the canvas was developed like photographic paper. I bought a roll, built large trays for the liquids. I coated the wooden trays with swimming pool paint. I bolted the projector to the ceiling to get the distance I needed for the large-sized print I wanted. I exposed the pre-cut canvas to the light through the 35 mm negative. Since the distance from the projector to the canvas was more significant than usual, I had to expose the photo-canvas much longer––up to five minutes. I encountered my first problem when I poured the liquids into the baths, and after a few minutes in the red darkness, I fainted. The thud to the floor jolted me back to consciousness, and I immediately realized that the chemicals' fumes were noxious. I spent the following day installing a fan and a one-way vent in the blacked-out window.

I remember the incident. I do not remember it tempering your impulse to recklessly throw yourself into your work.

I had ideas that could only be done by me. Hands-on stuff. I exposed the photo-canvas to my image and then instead of developing it in the bath I laid out the canvas on the floor, dipped a fat brush in the developer and painted abstractly on the canvas, thick strokes, thin ones, drips here and there and so on. And as I expected here's what happened. Only in the areas where I had applied the developer with my brush did the image or part of the image appear. On other canvases I applied the developer on the exposed canvas with my hands and in some cases with my body.

Plainly your accident did not stop you from literally throwing yourself into your work! Do-it-yourself artistic experimentation rarely threatens life. Even flopping forward on typewriter keys late into the night can leave an impression but is almost never fatal. Covering yourself in developer, however, may have been over testing the boundaries?

So what? I was young, I was immortal. And this was also where we developed photographs for your plays, and where we forged your passport to get that kid out of Hungary. Remember?

I do remember. That was quite a caper. So yes, art could be life threatening. Maybe even lifesaving. Especially if you were working and writing in Eastern Europe where the 'lightness' of doing it yourself really was 'unbearable'. (I only recently discovered that Milan Kundera moved to Paris around the time we did. Just saying.) Anyway, your Faustian bet with your life began to pay off. Reputable art shows. I am thinking Galerie Stadler in Paris, here.

Oh, yes, things started to move. I had already exhibited my work in Madrid, at Juana Mordó, and later it was the Gimpel Fils gallery in London. Solo shows followed worldwide. I didn't make much money, but it was good for my ego. The problem was, as a painter, I was a darkroom wizard all right, but I was getting bored. I tried a few more things. But not so much in the darkroom.

I am not surprised. As stated, you bored easily.

I bought myself another second-hand camera but with a motorized forward drive and I could take continuous pictures, by keeping the release button pressed down. One day I taped the release button down, the camera started to take photos and I threw the camera up in the air. It twirled and twirled and I could hear the camera clicking away. I made sure to catch the camera when it fell back into my hand. The pictures were every which way, up and down, sky and buildings and the street and walls and windows, and some through windows where you could see people, just imagine you catch a murder scene, and so on. A flying chance-collage. Call it in the air? Didn't you write a play called that? *Call it in the Air?*

A novel. Later, in London. In hindsight, that's what it was: 'a flying chance-collage'. I don't recall you making any paintings with those aerial photographs.

No. Just experiments.

I should have insisted. I loved experiments; just to see what happened.

I would also cover the camera lens and manually wind the slide film all the way forward. Then I would uncover the lens, start turning my body holding the camera, steadily rewinding the slide film backward manually at the same time and keeping the view finder open. This way there was no separation of the slide film into frames. Once developed I had a slide about a meter long. Some parts of the slide were blurred, others clear. I had a panoramic view of the room or the street. The problem was how to mount such a wide and thin slide. I would need to build a light box a meter wide, three centimeters high and thick enough to hold a thin fluorescent light. It was expensive and too complicated. I went back to painting on canvas with acrylic, and then later with oil.

The work that came from those experiments are some of my favorites. As are your later experiments with X-rays and Braille.

I thought of collecting thousands of x-rays from hospitals and labs in Paris and exhibiting them on a back-lit museum floor, an x-ray carpet, and people would walk over them and look down at them. I wanted to call the show *Paris Malade*. A Baudelairean title if there ever was one. When I approached the Pompidou Center about this, they thought I was off my rocker. As to the Braille, my mother, who as you know was a writer, died legally blind. When I began the Braille paintings, I swear I didn't make the connection.

I still have one of the large paintings using those techniques from your series with rags. As well as many of the large black and white photographic prints we used as posters and announcements for my plays and performances. They are a little faded as is my memory, but they still capture the time, back then, when our work suddenly felt real. And meaningful. If not, at times, a step too far.

I don't know if I ever told you, but back in New York I applied for a Guggenheim grant to make a half square mile photograph. Using a product called Liquid Light. On a moonless and cloudy night, I would spray liquid light from a helicopter over a square mile of Death Valley, then still from the chopper, with a stabilizer project an image, any image, it didn't really matter, onto the desert sand for a while. The next step was spraying developer onto the desert, then stopper then fixer. Finally, I would film the resulting image on the sand as the winds in the following days erased the photo in the sand. The people at the Guggenheim politely told me I was nuts.

I am hazy on the Guggenheim grant refusal. But I do remember you describing the idea and the project. And, yes, absolutely you were nuts. And you were right to have been nuts. Remember the Hungarian Caper. That was nuts. Art, political idealism, and adventure rolled into one. We had to do something. We couldn't just look away. And your studio-dark room experiments, (not to mention your own passport laden life) came in handy.

We discovered that your Canadian passport picture only had an embossed stamp on it, but no color stamp. That made it easier to forge. I first carefully bleached off your photo, applied the Liquid Light mentioned above that made any paper surface light-sensitive, and then I printed the photo of our Romanian friend where your face had been. The embossment stamp, of course, remained perfect.

It sounds simple in retrospect. I wish it had been. But maybe we will save that for later.

Now that we're on passports I'll explain why I have four passports. The Iranian passport is clear, my father's Iranian, and after the US army drafted me and I fled to Paris, the Americans took my US passport away.

A healthy fear of death can come in handy—even if losing a passport was the price. As I was to learn as well.

I got the U.S. passport back later after the amnesty. After my children were born in France, I applied for French citizenship, which was a Kafkaesque process. And I had a right to a Mexican passport too because I was born there. I can even apply for a Filipino passport because my mother was born there. Her parents, who were from Kansas, were visiting Zamboanga to be precise, but I never followed up on that passport. A nowhere man, ergo Paris was a good fit.

Paris did pull your multiple identities together. But I do not understand the 'ergo'. Is there a reference here to the Beatles' song? I am pretty sure Paris was not a 'nowhere land', although the dreadful idea of 'nowhere plans for nobody' captured the nighttime doubts and fears accurately enough.

There were a lot of 'nowhere people' in Paris.

19.

Looking for Samuel Beckett

WORKING AT *CHEZ HAYNES* WAS a leap in the dark, unexpected, an ever-changing *tableau vivant*. It was theatre in so many ways, with no rehearsals. Every night brought something unexpected. With a little tweak here or there, drama could unfold.

Improvisation dominated. And sometimes a more brazen intervention helped: a note in the salad here, a shameless reservation prank there.

From the moment one walked in through the saloon doors, the place became a stage. There was even the raised alcove over to the left in the back.

The incomparable table five, slightly elevated, on its own platform. The best table in the house. In the 50's and 60's that 'stage' hosted some of the best musicians in Paris. Our performances were different, more personal indulgence than anything else. The theatre of mischief might be a kinder description. Whatever, they were frequently ludicrous, even absurd, but always fun. Well, almost always.

All of us had been thrown there, and we seemed to know what we were supposed to say. We were rarely at a loss for words, we were "on", it was "show time". I dislike Heidegger intensely, but his idea of *"Geworfenheit"*, being "thrown" into existence and being, applies here.

His life was the opposite. He never repented or apologized.

He was a fucking Nazi party member until the very end when the American GIs were crawling up his arse.

But 'thrown into mischief' appeals. Although Heidegger would not get it. The evil he was thrown into, then embraced, was not mischief and certainly not fun. Not even human. Except in the worst way possible.

We had all been thrown together at *Chez Haynes.* In retrospect theatre was unavoidable. Theatre seemed to pop up often, outside *Chez Haynes* too. I recall a dinner at Bentley's where one of his friends, a crazy woman, tried to cut off my ear. She thought I was Vincent. She was trying to remake art history. I pushed back my chair just in time and she fell to the ground.

You were talking about Van Gogh. Passionately as you always talked about art. I don't remember you saying anything particularly provocative, but she suddenly lunged at you. She snarled out something like 'You want to be Van Gogh?' and then the knife came out. I think wine played a part. But not the whole part.

Back to *Chez Haynes*. Leroy was an actor; we all knew he had acted in films. The film or play we were in every night was unrolling and nonstop. We had no idea what *séance* we were in.

Just to be clear, you are talking about the French meaning of *séance* here, meaning a sitting. We were not summoning up the dead.

Yes, the midnight show. Walk right in, folks! You'll be an extra. The plot? No idea.

In this we were following Leroy's lead. Leroy was the tsar of impromptu. He did not emerge from the back that often, but when he did—because a few friends or some self-styled 'bigwigs' were in town—it was an event; generally powered by drink. He would make his entrance from the back, crossing through the room to the bar murmuring preposterous comments in a medley of theatrical snorts and grumbles and huffs. Sometimes he stopped to make a sarcastic comment or give a mocking hello. Always followed with laughter. I especially remember a group of four impeccably dressed, wealthy black businessmen from New York who knew about the legend of Leroy and wanted to meet him: 'Leroy Haynes!' they insisted with reverence. When I relayed the message to Leroy—he was peeling onions in the back—he told me to tell them he wasn't in and wasn't coming in. Finally, after their third or fourth insistent plea, he came out dressed in full costume, his faded pink tee shirt, casual trousers combo, pulled up a chair, accepted their offer of a drink and plied their ears with increasingly louder and raunchier stories. All to their wild delight. Leroy knew his audience. The restaurant's best bottles flowed, the anecdotes flourished, and the laughter exploded. Everybody was thrilled and overjoyed. It was pure unadulterated 'theatre of Leroy'.

We would talk about theatre during our Sunday night Chinese dinners. With a few extra Tsing Tao beers, we discussed Martin Esslin's *Theatre of The Absurd*, dissected playwrights such as Ionesco, Albee, Wesker, Beckett, and poets and philosophers too.

Those were all-in seminars: poetry, art and philosophy, but theatre was a favorite. There were so many theatres in Paris then—of the absurd, of death, of cruelty, of the oppressed. We would endlessly discuss them, and not just in our Sunday Chinese restaurant near L'Odéon or in *Le Trafalgar, or* after 'performances' at *Chez Haynes*. They broke out wherever we were.

I had read somewhere that Beckett lived on the Boulevard Saint Jacques.

I think I mentioned it to you. I remember we talked about our heroes—you talked Picasso, I talked Beckett. I was a huge Beckett fan back then. I still am. He was about the age we are now. We knew he lived in Paris, but his address was a well-kept secret. Even by his first biographer, Deirdre Bair, who kept the address to herself. Bair published her biography of him in 1978 and I immediately bought it. I forked out what felt like a fortune for a hardcover copy. It was many, many years before I bought another hardcover book. But for Beckett? I didn't want to wait for the paperback. She did mention him living on Bd. St. Jacques. There was no specific address given, but there were clues. I cannot remember all of them, but there were enough hints to give an accurate idea of the building's location. It was near a Metro stop, which had to be Metro Saint Jacques, and she commented that his view looked down into *La Santé Prison*. He was in the 14th *arrondissement*, so not far away from me.

One Sunday you and I started looking for Beckett's apartment building. We began at Denfert Rochereau and worked our way east, toward Place d'Italie. In those days, you'll remember, there were no codes required to enter apartment buildings.

Not the outside door anyway. Delivery people still had to deliver.

We told ourselves that this search was absurd.

But not Godot absurd. We were not simply standing on the street, waiting to get lucky. (Sorry, I couldn't resist the gag.) I had done my research, such as it was. Today we might be called stalkers. On second thought, maybe absurd would have been appropriate. We were searching for the author of *Waiting for Godot* after all. And, we had no real idea what the point of doing so was, or even how many buildings we would have to try. (Now, as I write this, I am suddenly feeling a bit uncomfortable; a forlorn image of Vladimir and Estragon farcically standing on Boulevard Saint Jacques in my mind.) The irony never occurred to us back then.

The Boulevard Saint Jacques wasn't that long, it ended at Rue de la Santé. I forget where exactly, and after three or four attempts, we walked into a lobby, and read the names on the mailboxes. And there it was. Samuel Beckett.

It was not very many attempts. Two or three buildings at most. The clues worked. But the name was not Samuel Beckett, it was "S. Beckett" on a metal mailbox, in a bank of 16 or so similar mailboxes, on the right-hand side of the foyer as you entered.

I suggested we ring the buzzer, but after much discussion, we didn't ring. I changed my mind; it seemed invasive.

It would have been invasive. Totally. Still, maybe we should have.

Maybe Sam would answer the door and tell us to scram. Although I read years later, he was an amiable man; he would probably have talked to us a short while.

He only lived about 15 minutes' walk from me. I contemplated just passing by on occasion and waiting around to see if he came out. But I never did it. Not once. It was enough to have located him. To know he was nearby. So, I wasn't much of a stalker after all.

I saw Beckett once, a few years later, at the bus stop on the Rue Dauphine. I was standing next to him and didn't dare say hello. I told myself every Parisian *intéllo* must walk up to him and say something weird or silly or even nice. I was sure he'd heard all the variations. I said nothing. I didn't wait for the bus. Much later somebody who works in the theatre told me that Ionesco, who also lived in Paris at the time, was lonely in his old age. He would call his publisher

Gallimard to inquire if anybody had called for him. Despite his fame and his contributions to the theatre he was alone; he needed people to talk to, to know that some people enquired about him and hadn't forgotten him.

For all but a few, that is the writer's lot, the artists' fate. Even the celebrated are lonely in the grave. Of course, some—I'm looking at you Nietzsche—live posthumously. But that only has meaning during the fleeting days of pre-posthumous life.

Thinking back to those times and our numerous discussions, I realize that we were relatively isolated. We had come to Paris with no letters of introduction, we knew nobody in the theatre or art world in Paris. We had arrived in Paris cold, with no connections of any kind to people who might appreciate our intelligence and gifts.

When I first arrived in Paris, rumors of intelligence or special 'gifts' would have been greatly exaggerated. As they would today.

I wouldn't go that far, *mon ami.*

20.

American Infantilism and the Communists

We read incredible amounts of books, poetry, philosophy, theatre, novels, history--you'd think somebody would appreciate our potential.

Appreciation! For reading and having ideas? Not likely. Everyone read and had ideas.

To make any headway, ours had to be the straightforward approach, knocking on doors. Who are you? What do you want? And finally, we did it ourselves. And I went to galleries with my slides.

And you were successful. I remember your first show at Galerie Stadler in Saint Germain de Près.

You're somewhat confused here. My first show--the one with the little cardboard boxes--was at the Centre Culturel du Marais, on the Rue des Francs Bourgeois. I don't remember the canvases, but I remember the cardboard boxes. My first show at the Galerie Stadler on the Rue de Seine were photo-canvas works, and some had the word *Picnic* stenciled on the bottom, I think.

I forgot about the Centre Culturel du Marais. But I do have a faint memory that the title, or the theme, of that first show at the Centre Culturel du Marais was *Picnic*. It was a solo show, a fair number of large paintings which picked up the idea of a menacing incident in the park, with familiar picnic items like the grass, a picnic basket, but also with unfamiliar items like a gun and suggestions of a murder or violent death. You wanted the invitations for the *vernissage*, to be unique and to echo the odd items at a picnic. You persuaded the Centre to put some of the invitations in small cardboard boxes. Fifty or so miniature "picnic" boxes were made up. Aside from the invitation, the box had a grass green bottom inside and you put in some small objects which suggested the locale in the park: leaves, small branches, pebbles. We went out one afternoon to collect some of these small objects. I think you may have regretted inviting me along and telling me to find whatever I thought suggested a picnic. After the first dozen boxes or so, I suddenly hit on the idea of adding dried dog turds. Who doesn't appreciate a well-formed turd? It was Paris after all. Dog poo was pretty much everywhere at that time. Some were flushed away in the daily flooding of the gutters, but many were not. You resisted the idea, but I was persuasive. (I am sure in your heart you knew it was a superb idea?) I collected a few of the very driest ones and we took them back to your studio. They had long lost their smell but to make it more palatable (and hygienic) we spray painted them black, so they were entirely sealed. In the end I think you hesitantly put them in about five boxes. I cannot remember what you said to the gallery if anything. I think you saved those boxes for some of the invitees you could be assured would not be horrified or sue you.

How can I forget that turd-o-rama? I found a wholesale place where I bought over a hundred little cardboard boxes. We spray-painted PICNIC on all of them, and as you say, we filled them with all kinds of doodads. We placed them on the floor, in no pattern, about two feet apart, and visually when you walked in, it all looked mysterious. It was an installation piece before it was fashionable. I forget what thoughts were behind all this; I had used the word PICNIC on some of my paintings in New York. But here, I had no idea what I was doing, and the gallery owner was polite enough not to ask any questions. He, erroneously, respected artists too much. Art dealers, especially young ones, think artistes know best. They don't. Most young artists are loud, confident, and wrong. I know, I've been there. I forget if there was an opening. We were probably stoned, so I have forgotten everything.

No doubt we were stoned. But I am certain there was an event of some kind. I can rouse a memory of it. It is when I learned that in Paris an art show opening is called a *vernissage*. A varnishing. Not something you quickly forget. And my recollection comes with the quality of 'varnishing' any memory still standing at our age displays: blurred, suspect, only vaguely possible, but absolutely true.

I held on to one of those cardboard boxes for years. I keep my sewing stuff in it, and whenever I mend something or sew on a button, I think of that installation.

Neither of us held onto one of those black turds. Except for the one that is exhibited in the Pompidou Centre, they are all gone. (OK that is a completely fabricated memory.) That show happened soon after we met, and the sheer thrill of watching you try something new and allowing me to add a crazy idea and see it materialize (even partially) was galvanizing. Limits and boundaries began to peel away; things became possible.

But we didn't stand still in those days. We were in a hurry and had energy, so much energy, and we used it, most often in a void. Somebody once said history is in a rush.

Just for the young.

We knew no influential people to give us traction. You went to theatres all over town, Greg, with your book of poetry *Tundra*, which you published yourself, and I did the cover for the book.

From the moment I arrived in Paris, I started writing poems. I was disciplined about that. I was under no illusion that I was going to make much selling poems or plays written in English to a French audience. But I was eager to do something with them. The incongruity of coming to Paris to write in English never seriously crossed my mind.

But you did say something important at the time. You argued, correctly in my opinion, that living in a non-English speaking country improved your English because you were spared the incessant ephemeral fads and fashions of English usage, generated by TV and radio and songs, foisted on the public. Living in a foreign country helped you taste and relish the words you used and read and wrote.

Hmm, interesting. I don't recall the language of TV and radio and ads bothering me too much one way or the other. I am sure I poked at the idea at some point just because that is what we did. But it was never a passion. Exploration was a passion. Experimentation was a passion. So, living in a different language environment led to challenging the idea of working with language in its common forms. I quickly realized I needed to go beyond the language of the text to get to the audience. At some point, I got it into my head that reading poems was not sufficient. They needed to be visualized and performed. I became evangelical about that. Even when I attended poetry readings in London the next year arguing with some established poets about it—Roger McGough comes to mind. And to perform, we needed spaces. Just as you artists needed your studios and galleries. So, you are right, we went to places and spaces all over town. Wherever we could get in, and when we couldn't, we created out own outlets.

Thinking back, we could have used a manager, somebody who knew about finding such places.

Word of mouth and friends were our manager. The *Colours of Power* recital was the first thing I publicly performed. There was a hand painted poster featuring a ray of light splitting into a spectrum on the edge of a razor blade. I performed it in a small space on the Quai d'Orsay.

The American Church?

Yes, that's it. I think they had a little studio space they used for music and small shows. The church also had a gym in the basement where several of us—you, Bentley, Scott, Kenneth, Vince and I and a few others, I can't remember all the names or faces—played basketball on Sunday afternoons. That is where your delusion of yourself as being a tall guy was shattered. Vince and Bentley put us both to shame. And it showed on the court. I am not sure if the basketball put me onto the studio space or vice versa. I do have a vague memory of working on stage with a black obelisk about Vince's height. Two meters.

The first rehearsal space was Bentley's painting studio. I think it was you who introduced me to Bentley. He was a young American artist, a little younger than me, who had studied with Willem de Kooning in New York. I remember he had some money, meaning he didn't have to work. For a while you and Bentley and I became a close threesome, to the despair of his French wife—it was she who coined the term 'American Infantilism' to describe our approach to life and work and art in Paris. We made a bit of an impact early on; a story, "The Three Musketeers" about the three of us was published in the *Paris Metro* magazine with the photo taken in your studio, the gun conveniently cropped out. Anyway, Bentley had a large painting studio in which we could rehearse. He also had a theatrical lineage—I think his father had been the lyricist for *Damn Yankees* on Broadway—and was interested in directing. Who was I to argue? We were all experimenting. And he was an enthusiastic collaborator.

Gotta hand it to Bentley, he really got into it, did his best.

The rehearsing was an interesting experience. He had a specific vision of how the poems should be spoken, which my acting ability was not achieving. Eventually, his solution was that I not only memorize the lines of poetry and the staging or blocking of my movements (which was relatively easy), but I also had to memorize a whole host of 'dots' which he inserted everywhere in the script between the words: one dot was a short pause; two dots was a medium pause, and three dots was a long pause. He was very dedicated to that technique. We worked on it for days, but I found it impossible. It felt stilted. Nevertheless, it was great performance research for me. It eventually led me to the more stripped-down, natural approach to acting I took to my theatre class and to future productions.

With Bentley, we started our own press. I collected some of those first poems, plus some new ones under the name *Tundra*; they were the first thing we published. A first (and only) run of 500—naïve optimism. I still have many left, but at 500 the unit price of the run dropped significantly. Thank God for Leroy. You designed the cover. A dark photo of an empty room. *A chambre de bonne?*

My studio, I think. But I'm not sure. That *chambre de bonne* was in a fancy building southwest off the Place Victor Hugo, and therefore had a radiator--in the up-market neighborhoods even the maids had the right to central heating. There was a tiny, one-person elevator going up to the fifth floor, and then you had to walk up one more flight. Most things had to be carried up by hand. Lot of floors. Lot of exercise.

I had forgotten that. I believe the photo was taken when you first moved in before you created your studio. It was empty except for the window, a black radiator beneath the window and a single sheet of paper, one corner slightly folded over, lying on the bare wooden floor. It captured the mood of the book perfectly. We called the press the Orléans Press and its address was Bentley's place at 16 Rue du Dragon in the 6th. I think the name of the press was my idea, but we kicked it around a bit first. It sounded professional and Porte d'Orléans was just down the street from me and one of the first entry points for the liberation of Paris in 1944. Orléans Press also published two short volumes of your poetry and photos: *Thirty Shots* 1978 and *Double Real Double Sink* 1979.

Sure, I printed the photos and typed all the pages for each booklet, and each was an edition of thirty. Small, I grant you, but a lot of typing, nevertheless. The energy we had! I also remember we talked about writers and poets who had started presses. Ferlinghetti, Anais Nin, Cesar Vallejo. I never told you, but in 1969 I mailed a postcard to Anais Nin's publisher. And she sent me a letter in reply. We started a correspondence of about ten letters.

You did tell me about your correspondence with Anais Nin. There was not much we didn't talk about back then.

I lost her letters when I left New York. I never tried to contact her again. I was turned off by her insinuations about sleeping with her father, a well-known Cuban pianist. Deidre Bair, by the way, also wrote Anais Nin's biography.

Our press and *Tundra* helped me to secure my next performance; at the Centre Culturel Canadien. You designed, Bentley directed, and Vince worked the lights. By then, I was not memorizing dots quite so intensely. It was a wonderful venue with a small theatre and gallery space and sizable membership list. Back then it was located at 5 Rue de Constantine in the seventh *arrondissement*. Very up market district, near Les Invalides. Amazing luck that they even listened to us. I had virtually no history, but based on a book of poems, a performance philosophy, youth and exuberance, (and being Canadian), they gave me a date. And they billed it as a performance and book launch. So, I sold quite a few copies to boot.

The oddest venue we snagged—I no longer have a clue as to how it came about; maybe they approached us—was a performance of *Tundra* at the Centre des Arts in St Germain-en-Laye, a Parisian suburb some distance to the west of the city. I remember telling the artistic director that although we employed music, movement, and lighting. it was all in English and it was poetry. They said, no problem, the audience would be high-school students studying English and they would be able to follow it. When we got there, it was a large auditorium. For this show we had added live music. Scott was playing guitar and Kenneth was playing piano. Each were following the music score by the light of a solitary candle.

I recall that Scott admired Henry Kissinger, ergo he was probably weird and right wing.

He could be a bit prickly. Whereas Kenneth always struck me as laid back. They flanked me on either side of the stage. The audience arrived and packed out the hall – a dozen teachers and 250 plus school kids, all nine or ten years old. We began. I completely lost their attention in the first 2 or 3 minutes. I tried stuff to engage them; like suddenly shouting out lines in strange voices. This halted the commotion for about a second, followed by waves of "ooohs and aaahs" in that young person mocking tone, magnified by hundreds of voices. Absurdly, we continued, as did they, a sea of kids talking and acting out to a determined trio performing poetry in a resounding vacuum. Scott told me later that near the end of the performance—when a teacher finally managed to battle his way up to the stage to shout that they couldn't hear a thing—he suddenly realized he had spent an hour playing his guitar for himself and a candle. He was not happy.

Weird. I wasn't there that day. It must have been nightmarish, one of those dreams from which you wake up and happily realize it wasn't real. But in your case, it was real, a nightmare inside out.

I think you were working the bar at *Chez Haynes* that day. Dealing with your own nightmarish kinds of audience. The moment was unsettling, to be sure, but the incongruity of the incident made it feel curious and strange more than maddening. The kids were the show. I should have taped it. I still have no idea why or how we came to be invited there. Saint-Germain-en-Laye was a communist run municipality at the time. We had asked the artistic director when we first visited the venue to discuss the details of the performance, if politics had any influence on what he chose to stage. He insisted the communist authorities never interfered with his artistic decisions. He had complete independence and autonomy. Although, he then admitted that he was a communist himself, so they didn't have to worry about his decisions or choices. How that mélange of politics and art led to us performing *Tundra* for school kids is still a mystery. We were clearly unorthodox (revolutionary?) on many levels and maybe that was enough. And, as far as I know, we didn't pose an anti-communist threat. Then, again, perhaps it was all a set up. We might have been invited and exposed to the students as a cautionary tale of what capitalist art run amuck can lead to.

21.

Black to Black

THEN THERE WAS THE PLAY, *Black to Black*. Leroy helped finance that from his winnings at the racetrack. He must have won big that first time. He gave us a wad of bills.

I don't think I knew that a gambling habit was behind the funds Leroy gave me with this play. Although, in retrospect, support from winnings at the track is more than apt. These projects of ours were all shots in the dark. Leroy appreciated the risk, the craziness, the art of what we were doing. He could relate. I think it was him through and through.

The creative life. The biggest gamble. The odds are slim. We found a basement where we rehearsed near the Place Clichy, behind the Cafe Wepler. It was a kind neighborhood, where socialist dreams met hopeful, poor creators, and wannabe bourgeois folk. I think Henry Miller mentions Cafe Wepler in his book *Quiet Days in Clichy*.

I remember it was a large, empty, decrepit space owned or leased by a group of young French artists and actors. They were a little bit older than us and were working in other parts of the building. The space hadn't been used in a long while and the first day we spent the whole morning picking up and sweeping the litter and dust left by previous tenants. After a few hours I asked one of the French artists if they had any large bags which we could put all the garbage into. He said he would buy the bags across the street and be right back. I remember waiting and waiting and wondering where he could possibly have got to. Finally, I went out into the street to find him. Across the street was a café. I went in and there he was sitting at a table with his colleagues having a full lunch. It was at that moment that I learned the culture of French meals. Two hours in the middle of the day to talk and drink and enjoy one's food. No matter what the urgency. Nothing is more urgent than a good meal. Certainly not bagging up rubbish. I was astounded at the time and feeling more than a bit irritated. Eventually I came to appreciate this lunch time break. During our rehearsals, we soon began to frequent the cheaper workmen's cafés in the area and enjoyed some of that same experience.

Do you recall there was a little restaurant called Casa Miguel near *Chez Haynes*? It was run by a Spanish anarchist refugee from the Spanish Civil War, and you paid what you could afford for your meal. *The Guinness Book of World Records* called it at the time the cheapest restaurant in the world. Quite amazing.

I do remember it. They served a full French meal with all the courses.

But back to the play. We scrounged up bits and pieces from dumpsites and empty lots for the stage set. Laura took photos, which came in handy since they provided a record of the permutations of our rehearsal spaces and the set too. We did this play with zero money, a play put on with leftovers. We created something with stuff that people threw away, death come to life again, resurrection. After all, isn't poetry made with leftovers?

The words for the play certainly were. Leftovers from some of my poems. And, of course, the set was. And, maybe, we were also leftovers as well. Leftover from whichever country or countries we came from. *Chez Haynes* was a curious community of young, mainly English-speaking, seekers, residing in Paris for all those reasons that inspire young people to see and experience and ride along with whatever is happening. We came from different backgrounds with different dreams and different interests and different talents but also a knack for doing things. When an opportunity emerged, we were willing to start sharing and connecting and throwing stuff into the cauldron. We provided each other with a ready ear for ideas with non-threatening feedback. I think we were all fortunate to have found each other. By this time, Molly and Tex, new members of the *Chez Haynes* crew, had joined the *Black to Black* production. Molly took over directing the piece. She had trained as a dancer and somewhere along the way had acquired theatre experience. She had actual experience directing actors in New York. I think she thought my theatre experiments were nuts, but she was also happy to go along with it all; and she added immensely to my performance. Later, she taught a dance course at the American Center, and I remember assisting her on a terrific dance piece which she designed and performed to Philip Glass music. And then there was Tex, who had no theatre experience that I knew of, but was smart, energetic, and happy to go wherever the set, lighting and stage management needed to go. He had also taken over Thomas' room next to me on the fifth-floor walk-up. The one with the shower stall. And you managed the publicity. Which meant photography.

Here, I want to say a few words again about taking photos in those days. Today people use their cell phone, and the pictures are good. They have little idea of what it meant to take pictures at that time. You had to use black and white 35 mm negative film. If you wanted color indoors, you had to have special lighting. We developed the negatives, then with a magnifying glass we chose the best images from the contact sheet and had them printed up. Later, as I said earlier, I set up my own darkroom.

I remember making those contact sheets in the darkroom. We poured over them, looking for the exact image that worked for our purposes. We did this almost from the beginning. For multiple shows. There is even a photo of the obelisk in my sitting room. We had cleared the room, filled it with dead leaves, and placed this obelisk next to the window. Don't ask me why. Maybe the leaves foreshadowed the rags to come. *Black to Black* grew out of the early performances of my *Jericho* poems at the International House, at 20 Passage Dauphine in Paris and at the Centre Culturel in St. Gratien, another Parisian suburb. I have little memory of how those shows came about and who was involved other than working with you on the photographic work. I do remember that the audiences were mainly French and working with a completely English text was unsatisfying. I gradually began breaking the poems down in rehearsals, improvisation and repetition of lines and movement, adding odd props—including a large electric typewriter and a camera on a tri-pod—so the text could all fit onto one page, be translated and put in the program. That is how *Black to Black* developed, the title coming from one of the *Jericho* poems. We were going to publish those poems in a small book, very similar to *Tundra* in look. It was a kind of sequel although very different poetically. You had designed the cover, with similar lettering over a photograph you had taken of what looked like an ancient Greek Theatre full of hundreds of empty fold-up chairs. But then events overtook us. It was not published.

Getting the play script photocopied wasn't that easy, there weren't that many copy machines around, and it was expensive to make copies.

I didn't need many copies to begin with as I had shortened it to fit on one page which was translated into French. We handed out both the English and French versions (and eventually German, as well) to audience members. The publicity package primarily consisted of photographs you had developed. Even the shortened text was photographed.

We got the package together, wrote a cover letter, and sent the envelope to the Edinburgh Theatre Festival. None of us believed anything would come of it, from Edinburgh. But a few weeks later they wrote back, telling us your play *Black to Black* had been accepted. You had been given a place in a Fringe theatre. The Fringe was like Off-Broadway. No connections to cultural power brokers, no brown-nosing the right people. They had accepted us cold. Because your play was good! For the record, for *la petite histoire* as the French say, I want to mention here that in 1966, when I was twenty and at the Cranbrook Academy of Art in Michigan, I won a playwriting competition sponsored by the University of Michigan at Ann Arbor. I went to some rehearsals of my play. But I never went to the opening night. My life was pretty rocky at the time, mainly because the U.S. Army was breathing down my neck. I fled to Paris. Recently I googled all this and to my great surprise I could find no mention of any kind of this event at Ann Arbor.

Most of this memoir will not be verifiable by google. All of it is from a time before Google. Before the days of endless 'evidence' and the historical 'authority' of the internet. Today, anything and everything can be found and verified whether it happened or not.

The play's title was *The Joy Boys.*

Prescient perhaps? Acceptance to the Fringe Festival back then was straight forward. If you could get a venue, you were in. Finding a decent venue was trickier. Ironically, it was the French aspect of our company and production that made it happen. Just as we created a press, we also created a little theatre company: *Alliance Théâtrale*—the name simply described this small alliance of different artists and actors and writers and dancer and technicians that connected in Paris at the time. I don't remember the details, but I learned there was a French Institute in Edinburgh with a performance space, so we packed up all our materials including a short performance history (replete with photos) and presented ourselves to them as a bona fide French company. Back then the French Institute was on Randolph Crescent, a very central location in Edinburgh. I know they had a huge number of different events scheduled during the festival, but they accepted us and gave us a good time slot. I think we had to pay something for the space, but it couldn't have worked out better. There were no high-level cultural world connections working behind the scenes. We just rolled the dice with the ideas and the art we had, and it paid off.

Leroy was our Maecenas, our Pigalle patron of the arts and of the poets. Leroy allowed us to be dreamers, follow our visions. I don't know if he'd like to be compared to the famous Roman benefactor of poets.

Hard to say what he would think. But it sounds appropriate enough. He had been doing it for decades with musicians and now with us. His 'patronage'—as unconventional as it was—cannot be underestimated. Not only did his restaurant connect us all, we always felt (but never knew for certain) that despite, or because of, the unique folly and madness that coursed through Leroy's veins back then, that deep down he appreciated, even cheered, the strange folly and madness coursing through ours. It's why we worked there for as long as we did. To support and feed that folly. I know when I approached him for time off to go to the Edinburgh Fringe Festival—biggest theatre festival in the world, bigger even than the Avignon Festival which he would have known of—his natural generosity and theatrical predisposition immediately surfaced.

"I suppose you want some money for this production as well?" he said in his gruff, long-suffering voice.

"I'm not asking for that, but it would be nice," I said, or something to that effect. I was genuinely taken aback.

"Hmmmpfff" he grunted, or something to that effect, and stomped off.

But a few days later he handed me a wad of bills. I can't remember how much he gave us, but the banknotes were of the 100-franc denomination not the 10-franc bills we were used to. The budget was certainly of the bargain-basement kind—we slept on somebody's friends' floor in a small flat not far from Edinburgh Castle. (I remember they had a three-year-old daughter who kept saying to Tex "you talk funny, you talk funny, you do" in her own very strong Scottish accent.) The train fare, shipment of the set and room hire required real money which Leroy's contribution covered. Most importantly, Leroy let Molly, Tex and I take 10 days off in the middle of the summer tourist season to go up there. I am not sure he had thought it through. Not fully. Or maybe I was not entirely upfront that three of us were going. Whatever, he was irritated about the loss of staff when we returned. Maybe Don and the manageress had gotten their grumbles into his ear. The first day back, I remember him saying "I hope you had a good time up there. Go ahead and take another week off," which he knew I could ill afford. Back then 'no work-no pay' was the rule for workers with no papers, and I had returned dead broke.

For me Leroy was always a bit of a mystery. Sure, I knew about parts of his life, but only parts, like snippets of a film. I never saw Leroy cry, for example. He had a diamond hard core. He'd seen too much, probably in the war in the Pacific. He could be very tough, especially on the waitresses, when he was drunk.

True. He had his dark side. Which was born somewhere we did not know or understand. The week following our return was tight. I guess Leroy felt I had a little lesson in life to learn. Baguettes and butter kept me alive. And 1F60-liter bottles of Ober Pils beer. But he didn't fire me. Which he often did with staff at the drop of a hat. He had once fired me for a month (no memory why) but this time I escaped that fate. So, the lesson was not as bad as it could have been. He was clearly pleased, although never overtly so, with what we were all doing, and I think the fact that we won a coveted 'Fringe First Award' made him all the prouder.

Given its experimental nature, *Black to Black* had quite a run after

Edinburgh, in a variety of different spaces and theatres in Paris; and then special invitations to festivals in Switzerland and Lyon. Then, along with *One Day in May*, it was eventually published back in Toronto in a Canadian Playwright series.

22.

Quoth the Raven

In a way, every evening was a new scene, in a new act at the *Chez Haynes* theatre. When would the curtain come down? After the waitresses had set the tables, and I had washed the glasses and restocked the bar, we sat down for dinner, and it was always plentiful.

And we could eat anything on the menu. Nothing was held back from us. Whatever we wanted. Except the 'chitlins' which as far I remember none of us was capable of eating.

Again, looking back, the times were generous. We ate dinner for free, and that was important for me. It may be hard to imagine but the money saved was crucial, as I'm sure it was for the others there. It was another example of Leroy helping me survive and paint. I didn't have to worry about scrounging up a meal in the evening.

It is worth saying again. When he told me to take a week off, it was the meals and dinner time I missed the most. We were young and burning calories in all the worst ways. We needed that food. And the camaraderie. Those meals were tremendous moments of friendship and relaxation.

The dinners were also moments of détente, when we were relaxed, and we talked openly about our lives or what was troubling us. But once the clients started arriving at seven, we all, except the dishwasher, had to be 'on'.

'Except the dishwasher?' You might want to ask Tex or check your own memory as the dishwasher.

It was showtime; no whining, no wearing your heart on your sleeve, you had to perform for the clients. And the client was always right, unlike French eateries where the client was never right. Put on a happy face and suck it in. The behavior of some clients was insulting and vulgar. I promised myself then that I would never ball out a waitress or a waiter for an unwitting mistake. And I never have. I saw how the staff worked, hurrying back and forth to the kitchen for the dishes, and then to the bar for the drinks.

I had my audience back there. Don and Leroy. They could be a tough audience, including throwing vegetables at the 'performer' when unhappy with the performance. Admittedly they were not a big audience, but they were highly opinionated and capable of firing the cast.

You must have seen a different side of the clients because they had to pass you washing the dishes at the sink when they went to the toilet. What were they like, were they in a rush? Could you hear them peeing and pooping or vomiting, did you ever strike up a conversation with anybody, did some clients have an obvious problem? Did you notice if any went again and again to the toilet? Kidney stones? Diarrhea? When you're heading for the bathroom, you can't put on the snobby or haughty face. You're on your way, most probably, to pulling down your pants and underwear.

Neither I, nor the clients, were at our best as they dropped by to look for the toilet. I was in a sink-soaked apron, most likely with sweat on my face. They were in more chic attire but, as you say, about to drop or lift part of their outfit in the one on-going, everyday activity that brings about that wonderful pleasure we never discuss. They rarely stopped to talk, and when they did, it was never to discuss the merits and shortcomings of urination, defecation, or vomiting. Those who knew where the toilet was, knew what they were in for. A tiny, squalid bowl, tank, and chain behind a thin door, just past a little sink and mirror in a curtained nook next to the kitchen. By the time they entered the back corridor, they had steeled themselves for the experience, and idle chat with the kitchen urchin who looked like the human equivalent of the toilet was not on the agenda. It was an awkward 'pleasure' they quickly wished to dispense with, without discussion. The discourse from those who did not know where the toilet was, was more extensive; usually a one-word inquiry on the way in: 'toilet?', often asked with a clumsy grin. On the way out, they were silent, a dark 'quoth the raven' look in their eyes. Never more. Never more. Many, I am sure, held their function until they left. Some of course could not. Some could not even hold it in until they sat on or stood next to the bowl. That is where I came in.

You were on latrine duty, eh? I never had the pleasure, I must admit. Or my memory has blocked it out, probably in denial. Dirty toilet? Rafael! Get cracking? I probably nodded and did nothing. You seem to have been more conscientious.

Yup, during the night if something went terribly wrong. Fortunately, at the beginning and end of the night, the more regular cleaning was done by the waitresses. And, of course by Alecia, the early evening cleaner. The manageress ensured it was cleaned to a high standard. But some of the waitresses had their own standards. I remember Erin, a young waitress from Dublin, studying something esoteric somewhere in Paris. She was new to *Cbez Haynes* and either did not know what the usual cleaning product was or decided it was not sufficient and, on this evening, found a more powerful cleaner-disinfectant to clean everything in sight. Later, a few hours into the night, the waitresses began telling us that a few members of the 'audience' (as you describe them) were complaining that their bottoms, butts, and bums (and French equivalents) were burning. Suddenly, I had a long line of people—mainly women (including a waitress or two)—in some considerable discomfort obstructing the salad making corridor, impatiently waiting to wash themselves. Later, we identified the '*désinfectant coupable*' layered thickly on the toilet seat. As far as I know there were no major injuries or even complaints, nothing that got back to Leroy's ears. But I am convinced that many of our clients left the restaurant that night with a much deeper appreciation for *la toilette à la turque* and a burning 'quoth the raven' look etched into their minds. And behinds.

One evening I mentioned I had done opium for a while in the late sixties. Opium doesn't give you a great high of any kind, and the first times I smoked it I felt sick, but I got used to it because the drug made everything acceptable, the world wasn't going to collapse around you and crush you, the world was just neutral with an occasional twinkle and that made all your pain and worries painless, therefore bearable. And quitting opium hadn't been hard. The opium talk led to De Quincey and Edgar Allan Poe, both opium users, and to Poe's love poem *Annabel Lee* and of course *Quoth the Raven.* We discussed how difficult the French language was and how rude the Parisians were. They never made the slightest effort at trying to understand what you were trying to say. Basically, the Parisian attitude was: if you can't speak our wonderful Gallic tongue then 'get the fuck out of here'.

Speaking French fluently as a native was a wonderful linguistic accomplishment. Which to my unschooled ear, you achieved as well as any foreigner, that, and the other half dozen languages you learned with ease, and apparently with an opium chaser. On the other hand, I completely agree with Parisians about the sounds uttered by my artless attempts at their language. I mean, how often can you listen to 'under the mountain' from a customer ordering a baguette and not shout 'get the fuck out of here'. Their rudeness was entirely *'compréhensible'*, and if it doubled as the bedrock of my liberty to do street theatre or engage in 'American infantilism', all the better. *'Vive Paris!'*

You had the gift of turning most dinners into a laughing fest. Leroy and Don emerged from the kitchen and joined in telling us funny stories. Even the usually grim and taciturn Don would recount something funny, about his friend Wilfred who had been in Paris for years and never mastered an iota of the French language.

If I remember right, he was English and looked and moved a lot like Kramer from the TV show Seinfeld.

'I just don't get it. When I make a phone call', Wilfred would say, 'all they say on the other end is 'nikity paw, nikity paw', which was really *ne quittez pas, ne quittez pas.* Or hold the line.

'Get the fuck out of here!'

23.

Operation Jungle Book

SO, TO THE HUNGARIAN CAPER.

Hungarian? I thought it was the Romanian caper. I remember exactly how I forged your Canadian passport, as mentioned above. I bleached out your mug shot and replaced it with the Romanian's.

Here's my memory of the caper, somewhat massaged by the fog of time. But, when I went behind the Iron Curtain, I was clear about what country I was in. Hungary. But with a Romanian twist. It all started when my friend Darian, the Canadian studying in Bordeaux, arrived in Paris. He had Hungarian descent and had just returned from a trip to Budapest to visit cousins. One evening we were hanging out in my rooms, and Darian was telling a bunch of us about travelling in a communist country and sharing some photos he had taken. Going through the photos, it quickly became apparent that one of his cousins (let's call him Janos), looked a lot like me. I mean a lot like me. He was a bit fuller in the face and cut his hair differently, but the rest of his features were mine. Then Darian told us his story. Janos was a Transylvanian theological student, not exactly a modern-day Dracula, who was, nevertheless, being persecuted for his beliefs. He was rather desperate to escape Romania and the rule of Ceaușescu, ruthless even by the standards of Eastern European communist dictators of the day. Back then it was difficult for Romanians to travel, even to neighboring communist countries. But Janos had obtained a week-long visa to meet with family in Hungary. After some more wine and discussion, we hatched a plan to help him. It was quite simple. And this is where your photographic skills and techniques came in.

It was pretty clever, if I do say so myself.

It was, and after that the rest seemed simple. Darian drives to Budapest, gives Janus my passport with his photo and drives out. Unfortunately, both the plan and the photographic technique were a little trickier than we thought. For the passport to formally come out (whoever was holding it) it was going to formally have to go in. Plus, we discovered Canada was now using red and blue ink in its passport stamps. So, onto plan two. You doctored a passport photo of me to look like Janos—we put bread in my cheeks and cut my hair like his. But still me. I submitted the photo along with an application for a new passport at the Canadian Embassy in Paris. That worked like a charm. The photo looked like both of us. It would get me in and him out. But now I would also need to go and give my passport to Janos so that he could leave with Darian. I would give them three hours to drive to the border and exit, then I would go to the Canadian embassy in Budapest, tell them my passport was lost or stolen, be directed to the police and after some administrative questioning would (miraculously) be given travel documents to leave. Even the best plans need a miracle. Darian got the okay for the plan from his cousins, so we were on. Like you, Darian had a car, an old Alpha Romeo which he called Julia.

Yeah, Julia, after the Alfa Romeo model called Giulietta. I found it odd that he could afford such a snazzy car.

It was an old, second-hand version. Not as bad as Leroy's Jesus, but hopefully just as blessed. We only had enough western currency to buy gas to get there and back. But we had lots of Hungarian Forints in our shoes which Darian's father had given him. So, off we set, driving through France, Germany, and Austria to the Hungarian border on what Darian had come to label 'Operation Jungle Book' after the famous book/film of the same name about a black panther and a sloth bear rescuing a boy-child raised in the jungle. I can't say our rescue operation made a lot more sense. Anyway, about a kilometer from the Austrian/Hungarian border, we thought it might be a good idea if I did not go through the control point with him. Not if I was to claim my passport was stolen; and not if Darian and Janos were stopped on the way out and it turns out the man who drove me in is also driving out the man who stole my passport. (Maybe a coincidence too far?) So, I got out of Julia and walked to the border. Five-meter-high barbed wire fences stretched out from the control point as far as I could see. I presented myself as a hitchhiker. The border guards, all carrying heavy-duty rifles and automatic machine guns, were not impressed. A western hitchhiker simply walking into their domain presented them with a dilemma. Eventually they allowed me to pass if I accepted a ride in a passing car. I resisted the car they suggested because the driver who offered to give me a lift—another Hungarian Canadian it turned out—was not going directly to Budapest.

I don't remember this at all.

You did not come. But you must remember. Your girlfriend and future wife knew someone in the U.S. State Department, and she telephoned her friend to get some advice. After a few words, her friend said 'stop, don't tell me any more about it.' So, she didn't.

This was a little live ammo training. The U.S State Department security could be listening to the call, even the Russians might be listening in, as I suspect State also listens to Russian embassy calls in and out. After all, paranoia is a euphemism for reality. They were all spying on each other, that was the norm.

In hindsight, it feels less daring than foolish. But when did that stop us? It was just another production, albeit with a socio-political-ethical twist. And some risk. This time the communists were not inviting us in.

The gift of the gab with the border patrol. Impressive. Nowadays they'd give you a cavity search with chain-link gloves. Just for looking suspicious.

And that's getting back into your own country. Anyway, I accepted the ride and the guards let me through, *sans* the cavity probe. After oddly resisting his offer of a lift, however, I think my fellow countryman was regretting his offer. He stopped at the border bar and bought us both a strong Hungarian brandy. More for him than me. Eventually, we started out down the highway, largely in silence, submerged in the lovely countryside of Marxist-Leninism. Sure enough, about halfway to Budapest the driver turned to Lake Balaton, which I learned was a popular tourist destination for Hungarians. He happily left me on the side of the road. I stuck out my thumb and waited. No luck. Finally, a long time later, Julia appeared over the horizon. Darian had been delayed with a car search. But we were back on track. When I finally met Janos, we both immediately saw there was a problem. This was not my twin I was looking at. The differences between us were more substantial than his photograph had suggested. He might get out if they didn't check the passport photo too closely. More importantly, during the intervening weeks, Janos got cold feet. Understandably so. When he ran the plan past some trusted elders in his Transylvanian town, he was told Ceaușescu would persecute his parents if he escaped. And there was also a little thing about a new girlfriend to contend with. Operation Jungle Book was terminated. My being became lighter and more bearable. I still think using our creative ideas and techniques to address the broader political issues of the day was worthy, if a little naïve. Or stupid. Maybe blind luck was watching over us.

Absolutely.

You know, of course, if I had been arrested, I would have given up your name in a heartbeat. Even if they didn't ask me.

Well, gosh Greg, that's generous. We wouldn't want your heart missing a beat, would we now?

Art deserves to be credited.

Having the Romanian or Hungarian police tie juiced electrodes to my balls would have been indeed memorable. Performance art they'd call it today.

The week in Budapest with Darian's cousins was eye-opening and fun. So, it was not a lost cause. (A quick footnote: Janus did eventually leave, after the Iron Curtain opened in 1989.)

24.

The Secrets of the cave

It was a little hazardous going down to the *cave* or coming up the steep stairs from the basement, lugging up the cases of beer and wine. I would place a table by the trap door in the floor so nobody would fall down the steps and end up in the hospital. In the dark my fingers groped for the light switch. The *fluos* lit up, and I was in Leroy's treasure den. Years and years of collecting wines that nobody ever drank. I think Leroy just bought them because he could. He himself rarely touched the stuff. He was a hard liquor man, as I said before. Thousands of bottles, red and white and rosé wines, from all over Europe, mainly France, Italy, and Spain.

La cave was a world unto itself. In hindsight, I wish I had explored it more than I did. Of course, I had searched through the different boxes and shelves for vintage wines listed on the menu, but so rarely ordered. To begin with I had no idea where to look. I remember even Leroy had to hunt a bit. For a special guest. Or a special event. Sometimes he would suddenly surface and serve us a twenty-five-year-old Chateaux Mouton Rothchild of some description for Thanksgiving or Christmas dinner. It tasted wonderful because of the story he added about how rare it was and when, where, and how he came by it. Would it taste any better today, after 45 years of enjoying wine? I don't think so. Not without the story. But I think I would enjoy *la cave* more. I would have a better appreciation for the wide variety of vintages and dates that he kept down there. At twenty-five when my experience of alcohol was still rigidly stuck in the narrow domain of beer—actually, just cold lager—subtle distinctions between different wines were beyond me. The red, white, rose division I quickly mastered. I liked red, tolerated white and hated rose. And sparkling anything (especially Champagne) was simply grotesque. I did immediately appreciate the simplicity and the excellence of the *Chez Haynes* Reserve; red, dry and 13F a bottle. Rumored to be satisfactory by the day-to-day client, but not worthy of a swish and a sip by the aficionado. Even the inexperienced, self-described enthusiast looked down on it with contempt, unless furtively served in a glass with the suggestion that it was a unique and ancient selection from the darker corners of Leroy's collection. Then its taste blossomed.

I can't help butting in here.

Butt away. That's the essence of a dialogue.

Leroy once said you can drive around the country, and search for small little known *vignobles*, and taste and search and retaste, until you're blue in the face, but the best rule of thumb is always this: if it's expensive it's very probably very good. That was also Astrid's advice to smart-ass clients.

So, not the timeworn wine rule of thumb: 'the older the wine, the better'. Which is the only decree about wine that I carried to France with me. And which got me into some trouble. The local Louis Max wine merchant who sold us much of our wine, gave me a real-world lesson in wine myth. He came through the door just after 5 p.m. on December 30th, 1977, just as he had on many other occasions, and casually sold me 12 cases of Beaujolais Nouveau. I had resisted because we were not running low. 'Buy it now', he told me. 'The next batch will be next year's vintage'. Despite the glaring clue in the name, he persuaded me with the 'age' myth. How was I supposed to know that Beaujolais Nouveau needed to be consumed in the year the grapes were picked? I had essentially purchased 144 bottles of undrinkable swill. When Leroy went down into the cave that day or the next, he was apoplectic. "What fucking idiot bought all this?" he shouted up the stairs. Leroy never let me forget that mistake. It took me years to sell it all––mainly to American and English tourists who knew less about wine than I did.

There was the lingo that went with wine tasting. We heard it often enough from wine lovers––oenophiles sounds better, eh?

Sounds rather grotesque and creepy if I am to be honest.

The men tried to impress the ladies. We on the staff just raised our eyes and said 'oh, oh, another major bullshitter'. Few simply said, '*ahh, c'est un excellent vin*'. Oh no, most of them had to embellish with comments about *le bouquet, la robe, les larmes, la belle attaque, la couleur,* and tra-la-la. There were champagnes too, but they weren't that old, as vintage bottles kept a maximum of ten years. That's what Leroy told me one evening when he came down to the cave and opened the freezer.

The freezer? He was in search of his special vintage.

The freezer was a big box about the size of a single bed. It was empty or nearly empty. In the corner was a frosty, brown block of something, the size of a brick. 'Give me the axe there in the corner, will you please,' Leroy told me. He took the block out of the freezer and placed it on the floor. He swung the axe downward, and a small piece came away from the frozen block, about the size of an ice cube. Leroy put the block back in the freezer and slammed the door down. He picked up the piece from the floor.

"What is it?" I asked.

"Hash," he said, "my hash stash."

That was his secret *Chez Haynes* reserve. But it was not for sale. I don't remember him often sharing it. We had to get our own.

After the wines, champagnes, and the beers, I took up the hard stuff, new bottles of the good liquor, single malts and blended. And middling quality booze, *Teachers, Black and White, Grants*. I simply refilled the bottles. If I ran out of one, I filled it up with another, same stuff, on different brand bottles. When Leroy went on a binge, I knew precisely what he drank. I became an expert with whiskies. When I ordered a scotch at another bar, I could tell after the first sip if the drink was watered down. And most bars water the scotch down. Leroy's cave wasn't my domain, but it felt like it. I would sit on the lower steps and imagine what an excellent hiding place this could be. There was a door, well encrusted in the brick wall, behind the pastis bottles. I never asked

Leroy where it led. Did anybody ever hide from the police here? How about during the war and the German occupation? Anybody die down here? Was anybody ever conceived here?

La cave did stimulate beyond its stimulants. Even in the middle of a search for a particular wine, it demanded you stop for a quick moment and look around. In the longer moments, after restocking and before dinner, you sometimes got to dream.

For dreaming there was also the cloakroom. It was to the left, at the back of the restaurant, after table five, right before you entered the kitchen. Sometimes when one of us was exhausted from partying the night before he or she would slink off to the cloakroom and take a snooze during the staff dinner. There was no bed in there, not even a tiny couch. Still, there always seemed to be some boxes or sacks or mysterious bundles handily plopped down or propped up to make a welcoming place for a quickie nap before work, especially on Saturday nights when Pigalle was jumping.

A snooze in the cloakroom after a Don dinner, and a long day surviving Paris, was a welcome reprieve. Even better late at night when the kitchen was quiet, and the guests were dithering over their cigarettes and coffee. It was a brief diversion from the kitchen, even if it was just sitting on a box, leaning back into the softest coat one could reach. Those experiences should be in Paris guidebooks, up there with a stroll across Pont Neuf, a croque monsieur in the Latin Quarter, or a glass of wine on any café terrace in the city.

The cloakroom was never empty, and apart from the junk that accumulated there, we found coats and scarves and gloves, and even a pair of trousers. Those pieces of clothing stayed there, sometimes for months on end, until somebody would come and ask if, by any chance, we had kept this or that. Once I found a bra and a pair of expensive high-heeled shoes. The lady must have walked out wearing only her stockings and raincoat. We were all sure that a few people had made love back there, but none of us saw anybody having sex there. Another thing I remember is that the cloakroom smelled nice. I can only explain it by the perfumes that lingered among the coats and scarves.

The odor was distinctive. That was partly due to its location next to the corridor leading to the kitchen. Not that the contrast with the myriad odors of the kitchen, wafting down the corridor, picking up the strong dark espresso machine aromas, was horrible. On many nights the combination was a delight; earthy, real, down to earth (pick your adjective), whereas the cloakroom was of another place and time. It took the lives of the clientele and concentrated it into a pleasurable, carefree out-on-the-town fragrance with just a hint of sex. And cigarette smoke (not quite the grotesque fiend it is currently). Regretfully, I don't think I took more than a couple of snoozes in the cloakroom: not like today when naps come fast and thick and are rarely perfumed.

I remember that I was nearly always a little tired, hungry, and cold. Nowadays some would quickly say, oh that's because you're not eating right, or you lack this or that vitamin, you should get your thyroid checked, you have low blood sugar. I didn't check anything. I was lucky, I was healthy, doing a hundred other things besides bartending at night in Pigalle.

Every night was late and often stimulant enhanced. Every morning was early (relatively speaking) to get a start on the real work of the day. It was a good thing we were young.

Much heavier tiredness invaded my body when I became a father. Feeding the baby in the middle of the night, emergency runs to the hospital, laundry, and more laundry, teething, fevers, and more. That was real fatigue, and it lasted the first ten years of my children's lives. That was normal. I don't care what people tell you, and if they tell you otherwise, they're lying.

What sane parent would tell you otherwise?

One of us would gently shake the snoozer in the cloakroom awake at five to seven, give her or him a cup of coffee right before the first clients walked through the saloon doors. Leroy knew about these catnaps before work, and he didn't mind. It is hard to imagine this easy-going attitude in a restaurant today, where every penny is counted in a computer and magically ends up in another computer in London or Shanghai. At *Chez Haynes*, employees had no precise job description, and we didn't have to punch into a computerized clock the moment we arrived. And when an accident happened, when I cut my finger on a broken glass, I knew somebody could take over the bar, and one of the waitresses would clean and bandage up my palm and Leroy, or Don would say, here, have some cognac, it'll help.

Yes, back to *la cave* once more for treatment.

The *cave* was our Lourdes.

25.

Running with the Bulls

We sometimes talked about death during those *Chez Haynes* dinners.

Oh yes, death. I will grant you that as a topic of conversation it surfaced easily. Sometimes too easily. It was a side dish for any and every subject. Mainly, I think, because it was mostly an abstract idea.

We were all creative people, and for me, death and creativity go hand in hand; it seemed normal to discuss our attitude and thoughts about the grim reaper. Eros and Thanatos. Love and death. And I'll add Techne and Thanatos. Art and death. Fearsome foursome.

Foursome? You counted death twice? Maybe not so surprising. It was a bit of an obsession for you. That may be why you took delight in a particular story, a true story, about my grandmother, which I told at the *Chez Haynes* dinner table one evening. Elderly and suffering from dementia, one very hot summer day Gramma walked off into the southern British Columbia hills to find her childhood farm. It was days before her body was found, by which time her head was missing, presumed taken by wolves. It was not until the following winter that trappers or hunters came across her head, much further into the hills and across the U.S. border. I think it was less the international dimension of her demise and more its macabre manner that enthralled your death-laden sense of humor.

At the time, I was twenty-nine, and as I said earlier, I was immortal--of course.

Yes, of course. We were all immortal then. Like every hale and hearty young person short on life experience. Nevertheless, late at night around the dinner table, we recognized there would come a time when we would no longer be immortal. And then the laughter came quickly.

Not all of us at the dinner table were atheists, and we discussed God along with death. That, too, seemed obvious.

That did sound obvious. But it did not protect us. Although, I was not an atheist back then. More agnostic with a lean towards Einstein's deity; not a believer in life after death. But I was always up for an on-going dinner seminar about God and death, and creativity with a bottle of Leroy's house reserve. Like any good Trinity, these three phenomena were conjoined in some meaningful way. Or so we thought. Although, we did not always agree. It changed from night to night and week to week. We poured over the distinctions in more detail and more often than I now feel it necessary, or have the passion, to endure. I think I have come to a truce with the universe: Creativity is overblown, death is inevitable, and God is the little elf that lives down the lane. But my time will come and, dementia permitting, I may undergo a conversion.

I told my close friends that since the age of ten, I had thought about death at least once a day, and on other days sometimes twice a day or more. I carried death around with me like a circus monkey on my back, or maybe like an addiction. That's what they called hard drug addiction in American slang. They said feed the monkey on your back. I mainlined my gorilla all right.

That is not so normal. 'Shooting-up' death sounds hardcore. Although that is precisely what a hardcore addiction is. In your case I was always surprised the monkey put up with you going straight to death without the prior accoutrement of needles, shots of after-shave or race-car driving. I mean even the monkey must have standards.

This makes me think of the few times Leroy would take me aside and say 'that guy at the bar, he's a junkie. Next time he comes around let me know, and I'll throw him out, I don't want him around, you can see it in their eyes, man, take a good look at him, you gotta learn to spot them, next thing you know they'll have their fucking dealers in here.' Leroy would go up to the junkie and tell him to leave. And the junkie would quietly walk out. It helped me understand that to open a restaurant and bar in Pigalle you had to be physically strong, make it known you weren't a wimp, a pushover. And Leroy, as you remember, was a big, strong man, period.

I don't think I ever learned to spot the junkies as well as you. Maybe you and Leroy had thrown them all out or had given *Chez Haynes* such a bad reputation for drug deals that they had stopped coming. More likely, I was happily serving them drinks in total oblivion. But we certainly had our fair share of night creatures come through the red curtain. They rarely got further than the bar, had a drink or two, fed a few coins to Genghis, and left. Death was seldom overtly on the menu. (Except for livestock. Then, it was the menu.)

My own death monkey was cute some days, and other days it was an orangutan clawing at my neck. I feared death, and the thought of it made me take risks as if in defiance, but it also kept me lucid.

Taking risks without death lurking in the picture somewhere, hardly counts as risk. And death without lucidity is unfortunate.

Why did I do self-destructive and dangerous things, the drugs, and the booze? I'll only talk about myself here. Sorry about that.

No problem. Self-destruction is a solo business.

The classical answer here, or the philosophical explanation, is that I wanted to risk my life so I could appreciate it more. Lame? I know, but that's the best I can come up with.

Not so lame. When you don't know how you are going to land, life can get exciting. Sometimes painful, sometimes exhilarating. Is the first self-destructive? Depends on the rage, denial, frustration, and nihilism that ignited it. On the other hand, mere curiosity also killed the cat.

If and when I hit ninety-two, then maybe I'll go back to all those things that aren't good for me, I'll even run with the bulls in Pamplona again. And I'll do drugs again, and drive fast, drink, and get stoned. This sounds pretty lame too, I know. And these days it smacks of machismo. It doesn't matter.

I am going to go out on a limb here and say that running with the bulls in your 90s would be more of the self-destructive vintage. Less being and more nothingness. Unless you have an overwhelming curiosity to learn what it's like to be gored, flipped 7 or 8 feet in the air and trampled by a dozen or so bellowing hooves. Makes sense now why you might want to wait until your nineties for that experience. Although, your 92-year-old self may have different thoughts.

Why ninety-two? Picasso died at ninety-two.

Then you want to hang on until 93. Picasso set scores of impossible achievements to surpass. He shouldn't get age as well. Even Shakespeare was humble in that regard. Only fifty-two. We shattered that achievement years ago.

But I never stopped painting or writing during that time, through the ups and downs. By that I mean since I high tailed it out of Detroit, diploma in hand, and came to Paris for the first time in 1968. There were lean years and--well, forget about the fat years. There weren't any.

Nor during our time at *Chez Haynes*. Although it was pretty fat on experience. Somehow, we survived self-destruction and rash curiosity back then, as well as their recurrent echo over the years. We entered the "settling down" phase of life—jobs, homes, relationships, kids. Now I suppose it's time to "bubble up" if that is a phase, or even a phrase. And do so before full senescence grabs us. Then all bets are off.

So, all in all, the very fact that we're talking now, that we're still alive in our seventies means that we've been fortunate.

I would concede that. Although I still hesitate to call the hair loss, the few extra pounds around the middle, and the loss of flexibility in the knees, fortunate.

Call it fate or destiny, or rusty joints, what you will. What did I know about death? I hadn't seen people blown up in battle and their limbs severed. I hadn't seen children dying of hunger or of the plague. Leroy had seen hard times as an African American in Georgia and Chicago, and later with army intelligence in the war. He sometimes told us bits of his life, and about the fighting in the Pacific. He saw plenty of death, and people wasting away of disease, infection, and sheer violence. In all my time at the bar, he must have talked about the war only two or three times. He never dragged out his stories, he told them as if he were reporting on the events.

Sometimes he embellished—usually with drama, humor and sorrow.

Our stories will always pale in comparison to Leroy's. However much we took risks and defied fortune to do its worst. And sometimes it did. Reality often rushed at us headlong in our own personal Pamplona; its hooves kicking back wildly, and frequently landing on us with a raw thud. But Leroy? His was a much more painful reality which we, through fate as you say, or good luck, avoided and could never fully understand.

I have seen four people die in my life so far, that's it. I want to recount this. The first man I saw die drowned off a beach in Mallorca. When they hauled him out, he was still alive and foaming at the mouth, as if he'd swallowed soap and not seawater. He died a few minutes later. I was eight years old. The second drowning was at the Lac de Vincennes, east of Paris, a young man it was, dressed in a suit face down in the water, and a doctor appeared and tried to resuscitate him, but it didn't work. I saw my third death when I was washing my hands in the toilet of a fancy bistro on the Champs, and an elderly man fell down the steep stairs and landed headfirst on the faucet of the sink. He was stuck there you could say. Awful, blood gushing from his forehead. The fourth death happened when I was driving at night in Mallorca. I saw some lights twinkling on the asphalt. I understood they were shards of a broken windshield. Two cars were in the ditch, both upside-down. The light inside was on and I saw a man with his neck gashed open. I told him I was going for help. He said, 'hurry up, *date prisa*', in Spanish, but when I got back fifteen minutes later, he was dead.

I have never seen anyone die. Not directly. The recently dead? Yes, of course I have seen them. My younger brother, which was tough. Tougher than I expected. It still lingers to this day. Other deaths I have witnessed at various funerals—but not my parents. Their coffins were closed. No one took their last breath while I looked on. I know it happens every minute of every day: in hospitals, on battle fields, in streets, in homes, on the highway. And now, even as we write, the pandemic is sweeping millions of lives into death. But I have mainly seen death mediated by time and through an electronic screen of some sort. I have not intentionally avoided it, but it has avoided me. I know it will not continue to do so. I am told it is a natural part of our being on this planet. Even when it is grotesquely unnatural and unfair. If I am lucky, I may witness the moments during which I pass, the few seconds just before it ends. Or maybe that would not be lucky. I have no idea. Despite the continuous irregular beat of my Paris-altered heart, I am, at 70, in reasonable health and all things being equal (which they never are) the sacred world of statistics gives me a few more decent years.

Now at seventy-five, I still think about death, but it doesn't scare me as much anymore. I've been extremely lucky. I've had a good run, should it end now. I have wonderful children, good friends, and I've said most of the things I wanted to say in my work. Of course, at the time, those years at *Chez Haynes*, I was taking everything for granted. A career? Security? The future? Never thought about it in earnest. Do all young people feel like that? I never asked myself if being a bartender was respectable, or where would I go from there? I didn't care what others thought of me. In a way I can't define, Paris was good for that kind of attitude. That doesn't mean that I liked Paris; it was a city that was hard but forgiving. There was the glitz of the Faubourg Saint Honoré, and the mean squalor of Barbès. To this day, I have a love-hate relationship with Paris. But the Paris I knew, and we knew, was not the Paris of Scott Fitzgerald and the Plaza Hotel, even if some of the clients at *Chez Haynes* stayed at the Plaza or other expensive hotels when they came to Paris.

Neither was it the Paris of George Orwell, even if we served their drinks and washed their dishes.

And few people, rich or not, asked me what I did besides tend bar, and looking back, why should they have? For me George Orwell and Henry Miller knew what it was to have little money. I know Henry Miller is considered a sexist writer today, not at all politically correct but there were some late nights in Paris when I would read him in bed and laugh out loud, his ranting and musings and digressions gave me hope and courage and a renewed will to live.

As is running with the ghosts of Paris in these pages.

26.

Art and Immortality at the Customs Depot

I TOOK YOU TO ART galleries some Saturday afternoons, before heading for *Chez Haynes*, and you, Greg, were clear-eyed and honest enough to look at contemporary art and make up your own mind. Something that I had forgotten to do. I was so involved in the contemporary art world racket and the latest trends that I had forgotten the bigger concerns about art, such as--did this or that work on the gallery wall enrich my life, or make me ask unanswerable questions, did it make me think and make me proud to belong to humanity?

I will always be thankful to you for these excursions. You certainly knew your stuff and were willing to share. I considered our many, many visits to art galleries, art fairs, vernissages as the equivalent of an advanced degree in art history and contemporary art. You must understand (as I know you do) before I came to Paris, I was a visual idiot. I had never engaged with any kind of meaningful art world. Indeed, I shunned it. Very early on, my schooling in art left me with the formidable idea that artistic talent lay entirely in how well one could reproduce the likeness of an object, a person, or a scene. Try as I may, I never got past drawing stick figures, differentiated in gender by a triangle at the waist and longer hair lines coming out of a roundish head with various circles and dots for eyes, nose and mouth. (Never any ears.) The utter failure of my eye-hand coordination, in contrast to my younger brother's innate painterly ease and dexterity, blocked my desire or interest in pursuing anything to do with art. The whole matter terrified and shamed me. To think I would one day have shows of my work (called performance art) in Paris galleries was the height of irony and lunacy at the same time.

I, on the other hand, was the eager beaver type. I was too often asking myself if this or that was truly cool, cutting edge. I was reading art magazines and probably not trusting my eyes the way I should have.

You always had a robust, critical, often cynical eye. Not only of individual works, which you could quickly and brilliantly assess and evaluate, but of the whole calling and the unpleasant business that wrapped around it. As I was busy learning about this new world, you were busy tearing it down. I couldn't have had a better teacher. I remember early on in our friendship driving with you in your old Volkswagen beetle to a French customs depot out somewhere in the wilderness of the Parisian banlieue. Orly, I think. You had just had an exhibition of your work in a gallery in Frankfurt or Hamburg, and two of your larger paintings—one and a half meters by one meter—were being returned to you still framed and still on their stretchers and in wooden crates. When you went to pick them up, the custom officer presented you with a huge bill for the import taxes. (This was long before the EU.) You were rightly outraged about paying taxes on your own work. He stood his bureaucratic ground. 'It is art, Monsieur. And therefore, of great value.' (We had to find the one custom officer who had visited the Louvre once too many times.) 'And certainly, worthy of taxes.' You recoiled. And objected.

Thinking back to such episodes I can't help asking myself––where did I get all that self-confidence? Illegally in Paris, one tough question from a bureaucrat, and I could get booted out of the country. You too for that matter.

The discussion escalated in volume and rhetoric with him eventually suggesting maybe you could pay half the taxes. If anything, you were more incensed. It wasn't about the money (which neither of us had in any case), it was about the whole idea of art and the art world and value and tax and corruption. You finally shouted at him that if he was going to insist you pay anything at all, he could keep the paintings. Indeed, you would cut them up into pieces right then and there. At that point, assuming he was dealing with a crazed Van Gogh complex, he finally relented and let you have them without paying any tax. Which was just as odd. Where are these worlds—filled with clear and firm rules coupled with the discretion to fully dispense with them at will—born?

We then had the problem of taking two large, carefully boxed, framed paintings back in your tiny VW beetle. We unboxed them, but still, they were not going to fit. At that point you had no patience for unframing and painstakingly pulling out all the staples attaching the canvas to the stretcher. You took out your boxcutter and immediately started slicing the canvases out of their frames. The custom officer was genuinely horrified. You tried to explain to him you were not destroying them, the art could easily afford an inch on each side of the canvas, but he was having none of it. He hurried away, muttering, and shaking his head, before the madness exploded further.

Of course! The poor customs official. I'm sure he regaled many an audience about the crazy artists he had to deal with, and how they might have killed him.

I'll give him his due. He believed in art, and he was not going to witness its destruction on his watch.

Now that we're on the subject of art, and many years have passed, and I have done some thinking about my career, I want to add a few thoughts here. I've had a modicum of success in the art world. Yet I often feel ashamed of being a painter these days, in the first quarter of the twenty-first century. I make paintings, I don't make art; it doesn't emerge from my hands the way Athena sprang, fully formed, from the head of Zeus. If I am lucky, some of my paintings may one day join the realm of art--give it a couple of hundred years or so. It's a long shot. Always was, always will be. Probably my paintings will end up in some garage sale.

Alongside my books. I am sure some of my books are there now. Others in garbage dumps. Some feeding weeds. Many, unwritten experiments never even made it to the page. But we keep on doing it. My writing took a long detour with academic publishers and journals. But your painting continued. You've been at it all this time. Successfully. Something kept you going.

Fear of total failure. What I, and not anybody else, define as failure.

Doggedness, even after I realized I was too old to die young.

That, perhaps, is the ultimate achievement—being too old to die young. It's really underrated.

Now I tell myself I'm so fucking old, people will say, hey it's time to buy this guy's work, he may croak any day now. He'll soon be on the wrong side of the grass.

On the other hand, if I may, selling after you have died? Really overrated. Especially for the dead artist.

Painting leads to unthinking my thinking or thinking my unthinking. But often, I have a brain in my gut and a gut in my brain. When little makes sense anymore, that's when I feel best about my work. But being senseless on purpose is being sensible, isn't it?

We did a lot of it. And it was fun. And fun is sensible, so, yes, I agree.

Nowadays, if you say you're an artist, chances are people will say, oh no, not another charlatan parading as an *artiste*—French pronunciation is a must here, please. Artists, I have found after fifty years of observation, are the most conformists of our cultural fauna. Gallery openings were usually extremely boring. As art world denizens know, only the losers looked at the works, while the others--sadly, often including myself--spent their time catering to the rich and mighty. Trapped in such situations, I sometimes did become aware of what I was doing and what I had become. I closed my eyes briefly and asked myself why on earth had I chosen to be a painter? When I was a boy, I wanted to become a bullfighter, as banal, and of course, politically incorrect, as that may sound. I played at bullfighting with the village boys, and later in my early twenties, perhaps in a last-ditch gesture to my childhood dreams, as mentioned above, I ran with the bulls in Pamplona every day during the week of the Feria of San Fermín. I still remember the ground trembling as the bulls thundered toward me, and I smelled the animals shitting themselves in fear. If you're a phony in the bullring, you die in under five minutes. In the modern art world, the phonies have taken over.

Art by its very nature is vulnerable. As are artists and writers and dancers and musicians of all stripes and colors. At least until it and they have 'made it'—whatever that means—and it and they can dictate their terms. Or 'pretend' to dictate their terms. They can speak for themselves on that issue. But all too much of it is abusive, parasitic, and exploitative.

From the very beginning, I wanted to leave my stamp on the cultural matrix of my time. A word to the wise guy: if, as a painter, immortality isn't high on your list, then you should do something else.

And that is the rub, so to speak. That 'stamp' and that 'immortality' is precisely what makes it so damn vulnerable. It's a wonderful high. But like those other 'highs', also false and dangerous. Whichever way you get your dose of immortality, it eventually comes to an end. It's hidden in the name, for God's sake: 'I'm-mortal'!!

Luckily, I had the stamina and perseverance necessary for the years of hard work required to learn the craft of painting. I was less prepared, however, to master the equally crucial craft of thinking for myself about art and unthinking and debunking most of the fashion-driven, historical, and theoretical claptrap I was taught in art school. I have become convinced through observation, reading, experience, and thinking that success in the art world today is based on luck. And you have to have the genes that make you a driven, self-disciplined, persevering, and thick-skinned person. Forget the talent; that's largely a romantic illusion. There is no cheap art, just cheap paintings. In art history books and university survey courses, students only see very expensive things. As for me, I am not looking for a style in my painting. Once I am dead, the art historians will find a style for me. Having a style is like wearing tinted glasses. Style is one more compromise. And fashion is a poor substitute for beauty. University art survey courses don't cover real history.

It's the grand collusion which somehow seems to work for the students, the teachers, the universities, and the public. But not always for the artist. I think I would say rarely for the artist.

Then there's the stuff no art history books discuss, the little nightmares outside the survey courses, but palpably present sometimes in the painter's life. Such as the cold. In my own existence after art school, the cold was poverty's twin those first winters without heating in Paris. I hated counting my pennies in the stores. Should I buy the warm shoes for the winter months ahead? How about a new pair of jeans?

For me, poverty was an only child. And the cold was a seasonal inconvenience. Of course, I was born north of North Dakota, and you south of New Mexico. The cold was frustrating, uncomfortable, but tolerable. Or I would not have stayed. It's not like I didn't have a choice. Gluing the sole back on my shoe to get another six months wear and pay the rent at the same time was just a problem-solving exercise in pursuing an ambition. Not real want or destitution. I do not remember gaining weight during that time, but I do not remember losing weight either.

Could I afford the large tube of titanium white or an extra meter of canvas? I peeled back the expenses in my life to a minimum. I discarded the canvas stretchers too and painted on canvas stapled to the wall or the floor. I rolled up my finished paintings and stored them in the corner of my studio, thus using less space and paying less rent. Only for exhibitions did I stretch my paintings. To this day, my relationship to my canvas remains intimate, like my relationship with my clothes and my skin. When I look at photographs of poor artists in the Paris of the early 20th century, I can't help asking myself who was paying for the smart suits and starched collars? There is no dignity in poverty, not even for painters.

But sacrifice sells. Like blood in a bullfight.

I know money is important. I have felt the sharp claw of its absence. Money provides me with time, light, space, heating, proper tools, and good materials.

What is it we used to say? Money isn't everything. But it buys better painkillers.

That wonderful phrase you coined. I have used it in many a discussion. That should be the motto over every art school. Money buys the best pain killers. Bar none. I have had to listen to aesthetes tell me that poverty is good for creativity. I have sat at dinner tables in posh restaurants and in designer-grubby lofts in New York and heard highly paid museum curators tell me that there is also something aesthetic to be found in Auschwitzian architecture. Other similar statements, such as Karl Heinz Stockhausen's quip that 9/11 was "the greatest work of art ever" or John Cage's glib remark that "there is just the right amount of suffering in the world", exemplify the despicable sanctification of aesthetics. Modern art has always suffered from a pedantic streak. The art world can be like sects riddled with culture apparatchiks. This mindset also favored the Romantic escapist ethics of accepting that the artist could be a child rapist by night and a sublime artist by day. I reject such ideas. Nobody should die for a comma or a color. The body is indivisible, and its movements and gestures, as a whole, make the work of art, from the synapses firing in the brain all the way to the hand holding the brush or the pen. As Gilbert Ryle says, there is no ghost in the machine. There is no soul, and I will add that there is no artistic *Doppelgänger* either. Declaring painting dead also rendered it self-conscious.

Delaroche's 1840 lament—the camera killed painting. I just looked it up. Although I am sure we talked about it around the dinner table of *Chez Haynes* or late at night at the bar after the restaurant had closed. I know you talked about it. Usually at some considerable length in one of your impassioned discourses that would suddenly erupt on the glaring sins of modern art.

Much of modern art is not only self-conscious but also dull and doctrinaire in the bargain. In a similar vein, the Romantics encouraged art as self-expression, a way of getting to know and heal oneself. I am not sure I want to find myself through painting or any other way. When you find yourself, you acquire character, they say, and when you have character, you become opinionated, and that's when you become a bore. This illusion was furthered by art for art's sake, a French *tour de passe-passe*, a meaningless soundbite. That would dovetail with the Duchampian idea that art could be anything you declared to be art. I believe in art for people's sake, which does not mean social realism or *Snow White and the Seven Tractors*. Art needs to generate meaning when it is shared. Every language has its own limits. That is why mementoes and monuments to tragedies and horror most often look flat, wanting, and ostentatious. People don't like to admit the limits of art, but they should. If you aim for immortality, aesthetics might be a matter of life and death for a painter, but it has nothing to do with human suffering on a horrific scale. And it is insignificant compared to the ordeals of survivors of the nationalist slaughters, genocidal wars, and slave labor camps that have defiled--and continue to defile--the world in my lifetime.

I remember when you raised these issues—grappling with the meta meaning of what you were doing, of what we were doing—the discussion would often shrink to an impassioned exchange between you and me. I never missed an opportunity, like now, to respond to something you said. Respond is too gentle a word. We would hurl thoughts at each other, 'full of sound and fury', that I recall signified something at the time, but often only to us. They frequently drove others away. Not that we noticed. Eventually even Leroy would tell us to get out and go home.

Suffering and art. My son Alex asked me: Would you eliminate suffering if the price were the elimination of art? He answers correctly, in my opinion, that there is no moral equivalence. How much suffering is a work of art worth? If the answer is not "none", then you eventually get to a point where it is morally acceptable to kill for art, a moral dead end.

It sounds a bit like the old woodchuck query: 'How much pain is a work of art worth if a work of art is worth pain?' Maybe none? But I hesitate to ask if any work of art has ever not caused pain at some point. But then, perhaps, we are talking here about grand suffering and the bargain with evil? If we are, then I would fully agree.

Much of what passes for painting today is mostly self-referential, or a mishmash of sidewalk philosophy, dime-store psychology, and barbershop agitprop. And I want to say here that I do not in any way accept the schizoid notion that *artistes* can be child murderers by night and sublime artists during the day. That is romantic claptrap. I draw the line at causing murder and death, à la Celine, who denounced Jews to the Nazis.

I am still saddened by how persistent the bargain with evil continues to be. Even when uncovered and brought out into the glaring light of day. Monuments, statues, artists, writers, actors, poets. It's almost as if the mystique of genius and beauty and, dare I say it, immortality, justifies its continued display and worship well beyond its proper place as historical footnote.

The potential, perfect communication in silence and darkness is not an option for me. In poetry, I read between the lines, and in the emptiness between the lines I find meaning beyond the words themselves. In painting, I see meaning between the layers of paint and between the brush strokes-- meaning that goes beyond paint. I try to look at paintings with no words left in my head. Communication is best in advertising. What you see is what you get, and you get it right away. In art, what you see is not what you get. If you are lucky, you'll get some of it now and more in, say, a hundred years. Thus, it turns out the dead do the best art. Do I need the nudge of death to squish paint around on a canvas? When I am painting, I suspect I am training for dying.

And there lies the seeds of our rift. It's still all too reverential for me. And I think the reverential is what I fear the most. If you fear the great nothingness of death, I fear the great plenitude of reverence. What if there is something eternal, immortal, and utterly sacrosanct? So, revered and venerated it can't be jeered at or teased or scorned? It becomes a lever for human harm. For evil. Which is where we agree. Looking back, the immortality and sanctification of Art and Literature have been the subtext of most of the longer debates and discussions we had over the many years we have known each other—starting that first night at the bar in *Chez Haynes.* We examined and re-examined what we were doing and why, sometimes bellowing and roaring at one another in such a way that others thought it would get physical. Which it never did and never would. I think we both relished it. I know I did. And you never refrained from initiating or engaging in the fray. Beneath the clamor and ruckus, we pursued the thinking of whatever we were thinking and the making of whatever we were making. Sure, the latter was often arduous and frustrating. But in the air was the dream of what might one day be. Art? Literature? After all, we were in Paris. But no, for me there was never an absolute. Painting and writing are never Art and Literature. Not in any superlative sense. (Not that I am fully immune to its appeal and influence. Oh, how I wish I was.) Those two imposters are simply passing edifices: built through privilege, luck, the test of time, or canonical decree. The purveyors of both—academic, merchant, dealer, agent, critic, investor, or whomever—desperately need to make a living and their reputation. Along the way they sometimes crush or inadvertently help a painter or poet to do the same.

I am always puzzled that film and stage directors, poets, dancers, singers, actors, and writers refer to themselves as just that. In contrast, painters and sculptors say they are artists, not painters or sculptors, as if they need the reassuring 'artist' label to be taken seriously--or perhaps take themselves seriously.

Good luck to them all—however they want to refer to themselves and their work. We usually tried not to be quite so serious. Back on the tarmac of the customs depot, you finished carving the canvasses (paintings? art?) from their frames and were about to roll them up and put them in your car. But there were a couple of lessons left to learn. Not about taxes, nor about the immortality of art. Just as we started rolling the paintings, you offered me one of the paintings for my help that day. It was a first-rate lesson on the value of friendship. You allowed me to choose. And I chose. Then came the second lesson. You immediately regretted giving me the choice. You had taught me well. Not all art is equal. I happened to choose the one you liked best. We flipped a coin and I won.

Painting is quite a ridiculous way to spend my life. Inspiration is like epilepsy; I fall flat on my face. My breathing is what is most articulate about me.

Or a heartbeat. Irregular and doomed.

Good symbol. Or metaphor. Doom. Boom. The last heartbeat is eternal but silent.

Unlike Art. Which dies with a whimper.

27.

A Fabulous Bubble

Art and love and women, we agreed about art most of the time, but love and women? Rarely.

You would have to remind me of what I believed back then and how we differed. But *sans* evidence, I would have said it was the other way around. Art? We rarely agreed. Not to begin with. I think you took it more seriously than I. Love and women. You may be right. Perhaps, I took it more seriously than you. But maybe not.

We might be wary of such talk now as old farts. A theme so thrashed and trashed and lauded and even deified in literature, we should stay away from it, that's what's going through my head.

Stay away from it. On that I do agree. Fully.

No need to make fools of ourselves, or of myself, once again.

Again, I absolutely agree.

But I might try?

So, again, this is where we diverge.

The little world at *Chez Haynes* was a microcosm of these feelings, wasn't it? Leroy had been married a few times. He loved women and hated them, and when he was drunk some evenings, he railed against women; how they had screwed him over, but that's neither here nor there. The bottom line was the hurt and pain.

It was both here and there for him. Whatever the exact nature of his pain, he suffered it in the way he lived life. Fully.

Same for Don, he wasn't with his woman anymore, and he had to see her every day, and we could see Don's anger at her. We all felt that he would defend her to the death if anyone tried to harm her. We never really knew what had happened between them. Who had been unfaithful? Who could forgive?

We knew who was hurting the most. Or who appeared to be hurting the most. Don. Not that we took sides. We stepped back and let it play out. Peacefully. Meaning with no violence to anyone. Maybe, you fueled the fire a wee bit. That is not a criticism. Their relationship was over. And no one was physically hurt. As far as I know.

And the waitresses? On slow nights we hung around the bar and drank and talked. Other nights at *Le Trafalgar* we'd let our hair down as they say--I had hair then.

I think that is all we had. But we had a lot of it.

Each waitress had a love story or two to tell. I did too, but I kept them discreet. I have never been the type to discuss affairs with anybody. I'm not going to start here.

Fair enough. It makes this chapter easier.

The love stories were from the past and never ended well, but I suppose love stories of the past never end well.

That is why they are in the past.

We talked about fidelity and money.

I remember talking about fidelity. But not so much about money; not in relation to fidelity.

What did we want? Security and ongoing commitment and a relationship? Even if the sex was no good?

I think we came from different vantage points back then. We probably disagreed about fidelity and sex. But maybe I am kidding myself.

The women were divided on this at the time, some said the commitment and the relationship were more important than the sex. Others claimed the opposite.

This sounds like the controversy about 'open relationships' which was circulating widely back then. We certainly discussed its merits and drawbacks at the *Chez Haynes* dinner table.

Fidelity was a different matter for each one. For a few of the waitresses, was infidelity par for the course? I won't hazard a guess.

Neither will I. But your question sounds like the kind of thing a man might have wished for back then. I guess I am not surprised about the lack of agreement in the sample of women you surveyed in your research.

Research? You're giving me more credit than I deserve. Most of the women wanted children one day; it was a subject that came up often. And children require commitment.

Children? I do not remember any conversation about having children. Certainly not with respect to fidelity or open relationships. But that may be selective forgetting on my part.

I may have brought it up, but no, children were too serious a responsibility for me to even imagine then in Paris. Later on, after the birth of my second child, I underwent a vasectomy. I was certain I would never have the means to support more than two children all the way through their college and graduate school studies.

Thoughts about having children were the furthest thing from my mind at that time. I knew I was not ready. I was barely ready to bring myself up. I left Canada and came back to Europe instead.

Looking back, I think I returned to Europe because I felt less of an exile here. It has nothing to do with passports. I think, at times, that exiles don't exist. They're a useful concept for people who exist in places between places. They don't have any coordinates, no national longitudes, and latitudes. Maybe this makes no sense, but it sounds good.

I am not sure one ever completely shakes off national longitudes and latitudes. We just acquire additional ones which helps smooth over some of the rougher patches. Like with love, sex, and relationships.

We didn't realize it in Paris then, but we were living in an incredible era of sexuality. The pill was easy to buy over the counter for women, abortion in France was on-demand and free. AIDS wasn't around. I didn't want a relationship; the very word scared me. I did not want to commit to any long-term arrangement.

That is where our thoughts did converge. Although I do not remember discussing it at the time. We just lived it.

To put it bluntly, it was a fabulous bubble in time when it came to sex.

A fabulous bubble. That would be a good name for this chapter.

Danger-free sex. And I liked living alone. Women were kind to me, generous, giving, and now, so many years later, I hope that they remember me that way too. Is that asking a lot?

It depends entirely on how you, we, behaved. In some cases, it might have been asking for much more than we deserved or had a right to hope for.

Probably. But then, as Auden writes, *hearts that we broke long ago, have long been breaking others.*

28.

La sagesse des *clodos*

As I mentioned before, *Chez Haynes* was well heated, but outside of *Chez Haynes*, everywhere I felt the cold seep right into my bones.

The local café was always a great place to escape the cold. Especially if the cold was accompanied by deep, penetrating rain. Warming up in a café with an espresso (never more than a franc) and people milling nearby, radiating their heat into the environment, was a surprisingly pleasant experience.

For some couples, for the bums in the subway, each person could be a heating source for the other. The metro was usually warm when the stations were underground, and that's why I never took the bus in winter. They weren't well-heated. I felt for the *clochards, les clodos*-—the beggars and the outcasts, who spent the days in the metro. They would find a spot either on the station platform or in the maze of corridors in the big stations like Chatelet or Montparnasse or République, where they spread out their blankets and pieces of cardboard and hopefully, a plastic bottle of *gros rouge*, the cheapest red wine. They set up house for the day. And some *clodos* were couples.

They, too, had found the secret of 'warmth'. People, shelter, a beverage of choice.

They dozed in their wine-induced stupor, but they were rarely asleep, for they always perked up enough to say *merci* when somebody gave them something, a coin or a little food, a baguette or a sausage or a *pâtisserie*. The homeless dreaded the often-fatal hour at zero-forty-five, a quarter to one in the morning when the last metro rumbled through and the metro staff, often accompanied by cops, would shoo the *clochards* out because the station was closing. The metro staff would then pull the door-grills shut at the stairs leading up to the street. The bums would sometimes settle in for the night by the grills because warm air seeped out and up from the metro tunnels. I say fatal because it was for some. When the temperature sank below zero Celsius, the cardboard and blankets and shared bodies weren't sufficient to keep them alive; often sick and always under-nourished, the *clochards* sometimes died, huddled by the grill gates of the metro, curled up in somebody's arms. A few times I witnessed city officials, with vans from the public shelters, come and offer to take the homeless to a warm place, a shelter, for the night. Most of the *clodos* refused to budge.

Shelter came with some severe strings attached. I remember the city eventually rounded them all up once a month, or thereabouts, to hose them down and disinfect them.

Yeah, that's why some of the *clodos* had dogs with them. With dogs the cops couldn't round them up.

Clever move. We could have learned more from the *clodos*. Like the homeless everywhere, there is often wisdom, *sagesse*, there.

The *clodos* insulted the officials who tried to help and got in a good attack on the president of the republic––'have you seen the president's shoes, his fucking suits and ties, do you know how much they cost, enough to keep me going for a year, and you're offering me a fleabag hotel?'

It wasn't much of an offer from the city. A decent pair of shoes would have made a difference. Some of them didn't have shoes, and the shoes the others wore didn't look like they fit or were even worthy of the name.

Shoes were a big thing for us too. They were expensive. Buying a new pair was a big event, they had to be affordable, a fancy word for cheap, and not just right for the winter but for the summer too. And how about a new pair of jeans?

Counting pennies, in this case bronze colored 5 and 10 centimes pieces, was second nature. It all added up. Making sure I had 40F for my *carte orange* and could pay my 500F rent at the end of the month was the goal. During the day, the metro was a godsend but sleeping overnight on its grates never looked that appealing. Everything else, including heat and clothes, fit in when and where possible. I remember oscillating between being one hundred francs up and one hundred francs down at the end of the month. If I went into the next month up, I was rich.

In my apartment, the two electric heaters were never powerful enough. I dreaded the electricity bill at the end of the month. I didn't want the power company to cut off the juice. That would be terrible. The windows in Parisian rooms were never double-glazed; this was a long time before the ecology issue became a global concern. Paris wasn't built for the cold. Some of our friends had coal stoves in their apartments, and the metal tube-chimney snaked out the window. The coal was delivered in sacks and placed outside the door. Sometimes at friends' apartments I would watch in admiration as the coal carriers huffed up the stairs with the sacks on their backs. The men's faces were blackened with coal dust. And the dust permeated the apartment, and lighting the stove in the morning, my friends told me, was a messy ritual. Others, including me, well, we cheated, as mentioned before, we lived in fear that the meter reader would show up unannounced and the fine would be huge, and the cops might get involved. That's why we spent so much time in cafes, mainly to keep warm. And at home I had extra blankets.

The coal men never went up the last flight of stairs in my building. No fireplaces in the servants' quarters. In any case, I rarely considered the weather a major cause of concern. Maybe that is the legacy of coming from a colder longitude and latitude. Plus, it rarely snowed in Paris in the winter. The weather didn't interrupt transportation. Believe me, that is a major plus for a city. And there were some benefits. The hordes of fair-weather sightseers were gone. So, I was not immediately regarded as a tourist. Which was always irritating. And sometimes you could get too much of a good thing. I am thinking here of the summer of 1976. There was a huge heat wave that year. I dread to think how the *clodos* fared. No rain for months. And no such thing as air conditioning. Liter bottles of cold Ober Pils lager saved me. I remember going to an outdoor municipal swimming pool one day just to avoid the heat. It was packed with Parisians *sans* their haute couture and fashion. (Speedos were never a good look.) At some point in the afternoon a few clouds unexpectedly appeared in the sky. Not rain clouds. Just clouds. Everyone in and out of the water suddenly burst into a loud spontaneous round of applause. I don't have any memory of a similar, unexpectedly cold winter spell in Paris. But, yes, I know there were some rough days, when I had my feet propped up in front of my little portable electric heater. Or when I went to bed with my clothes beside me under the blanket so they would be warm when I put them on the next morning. It was a frequent topic of conversation. I recall Laura and I discussing it more than once and in some detail. We compared the relative merits of heat and humidity versus cold and snow. She was from New Orleans and didn't like the cold either.

Warm clothing, which brings me to laundry.

Ahh, Laundry. Don't get me on to laundry. That was always an issue. Summer or winter.

When you don't have money, you wash your clothes by hand, with cold water. You never take anything to the dry cleaner, that's too expensive. I don't remember any laundromats, but there must have been some. It would be an excellent place to hang out and keep warm.

I did go to the laundromat. Underwear and socks were washable in the sink. But the bigger items? You needed a machine. So, I went. Not often but when the odor reached a certain point. It was a bit of a hike and I learned early on you needed to have the right change. And lots of it. The washing machines took one-franc coins and the dryers sucked in an endless stream of 50 centime pieces. The first time I quickly ran short of both one franc and half franc coins. So, I slipped next door to a café. I politely asked the cashier for change for 5 francs.

'Bonjour Madame. Est-ce-que vous avez de la monnaie pour cinq francs?'

'Non, monsieur.' she was instantly wagging her finger in my face. *'C'est pas une banque.'*

'Mais—'

'Allez monsieur. Ce n'est pas une banque.'

I could see that her till was loaded with coins. I was not asking to make change for a 100 franc note. just a 5-franc coin. It was like asking for a few quarters and dimes. But I suppose I was pushing the boundaries, asking for a small courtesy; less effort than it took her to tell me the café was not a bank. Maybe she was performing street art. *À la* Magritte. *'Ceci n'est pas une banque'*.

Do you mean the famous *"Ceci n'est pas une pipe"*? In French argot *une pipe* is a blowjob.

Yes, that was the reference. Without the *'pipe'* part. She never offered me that either. Next door in the launderette, I put in a little more soap and doubled the load in an already stuffed washing machine. For the next day or so, my clothes hung from my pull-out shower, from bookshelves, window handles and on a barely working radiator. She saved me a dollar or two, so maybe she did me a favor. She certainly reinforced my sense of liberty to behave however I wanted. Like the *clodos*. There may not have been much equality or fraternity in Paris, but liberty was running rampant.

29.

Square One

HEATING, CANVAS, CLOTHES, FOOD, PAINTS, books. And the car? Parking was free. I took out the cheapest insurance, third party insurance. I kept it down to basics. A portable cassette player, maybe?

I didn't know how you could afford your life. Running a car? I assumed you were rich—relatively speaking: a few hundred francs a month beyond my dreams. But then your painting began to make some money for you. You were exhibiting, solo shows at bona fide galleries on the Left Bank. And small red dots began to appear next to your paintings.

I had a little money, but it wasn't a state of mind. I went ahead with creative projects, such as your play. I say it wasn't a state of mind because I, and you too, had been lucky, we were educated, and in good health, and the lack of money was a small obstacle. It was, more than anything, a physical inconvenience. I could afford museums, the Louvre was free one day a week, I forget which. We were confident our lives would lead somewhere, money wouldn't always be a problem, although for me it did continue, but to a lesser degree. I was averaging two or three solo shows a year in Europe and America. I was making money. Ours was a confident generation.

Too confident sometimes. I think that began to change when the world didn't exactly turn out the way we all expected.

I want to emphasize luck. I was very lucky. I have met over my life many painters who are better than I am in all ways, better technically, with a more fertile imagination, hard-working and self-disciplined, and they have had no luck, haven't made it to square one.

Square one?

I am convinced there is a universe of great paintings that hasn't been 'discovered' by the critics and art historians and collectors. And probably never will.

Oh, that square one. Recognition. And a living. Or the skeleton of a living.

For some painters, bad luck grinds them into giving up, and I can't blame them. It's worse for sculptors. You do a few large pieces in stone and don't sell them? You have to move out soon, the sculptures take up all the living and working space. I am sure that was before today's conceptual sculpture, which presents no storage and transport issues and is very rarely any good. Sculptors had to find buyers or else they had to move or quit and moving implied already having money. Making sculptures you never sold drove you to quit doing it. Severe selection indeed.

Selection is always severe at the time. Less so in hindsight. I never experienced an existential state of poverty. A state of desperation and privation from which it was impossible to escape. We had a supportive community. That was lucky. And there was enough recognition and means of living that I was able to stay on square one for almost a decade. (Then my work and writing changed to a more life sustaining academic square one.) And, of course as you say, there was always the knowledge we could quit. Leave at any time. Get a 'real' job. It was always a topic of conversation. Many left, returned home.

Sadly, I couldn't go home. My father's pension was barely sufficient. I couldn't go home and live off my parents.

I eventually left Paris after four years. To carry on in London. Going home, meaning the place I came from, had to wait forty years. My parents had died by then.

Money, going home, was a constant source of worry. Leroy paid us in cash, which I kept on me most of the time. I did open a bank account in the end, for a silly reason: it made me feel more settled, rooted somehow. I needed roots. I had lived in Mexico, Spain, Austria, England, U.S., France. I know it's ridiculous, but that's what I needed. I had moved around so much that now I wanted to be settled. Look, see, I have a bank account, and I have my address. It's on my checkbook. It was easy opening a checking account, much easier than it is now, and even though I had a tiny balance, the bank told me I could overdraw too. Made me feel rich, that did. I didn't declare any tax information. Now I had a postal address, mailbox, and a bank account and even a checkbook. Wow! I was living in Paris. I wasn't legal in the least, but that didn't matter to me.

To begin with, cash was everything. We were solid members of the dark economy. Paid in cash and tips. Not that the tips were huge. I think, after we divided it up among the wait staff and the barman, it averaged 10F a piece a night. I remember the dishwasher was only paid 90 francs a night versus 100 francs for the waitresses and barman; no share in the tips for the kitchen staff which consisted of just me. When I finally transitioned to the bar, I lobbied hard for the dishwasher to be included. And he was. I had a small metal box under my bed which I would put money into to ensure the bills would be paid and projects save up for. A real bank account was not even on my horizon. But I do remember you getting an account and later a bank card. I remember the marvel of you going to what must have been one of the earliest ATMs in Paris to take out money. It looked like magic. In my last year, with the help of your recommendation and my *carte de séjour*, which I finally got in my last year, I also got a bank account. It felt so important and weighty that I did not give it up, or touch the money, until long after I left Paris. I finally closed it when I returned many years later with my wife. Still living on a tight budget, we were delighted to take the remaining 406F and feel exceedingly rich for a few days.

And getting mail was free too. That was something amazing, and sending letters was affordable. You can imagine the excitement of opening my mailbox in the morning and when I got home from *Chez Haynes* late at night. There were three mail deliveries a day then, in the seventies. Would there be a letter from a friend, a girlfriend, a love letter or even a photo?

There was something nice about having a mailbox. Not that I remember many letters from friends, lovers, or devoted fans. Some responses from theatres or a venue about a performance or an idea. Mainly rejections, but sometimes an opportunity as well. The bulk were of the everyday kind, reminders from the landlord, electricity bills and notices from the city and the local community. There was never a perfumed card with an invitation to afternoon tea. Although, I do remember a kind thank you card from your father for a book or something I had sent to him. On one of those literary cards with the sender's name formally embossed on it. Very nice.

I never knew this! That's quite something. Amazing, really. My father rarely wrote letters, and the few he wrote to me in Vienna or later in college were illegible. Hopefully you deciphered his.

I did. It was short. A sentence or two. Much appreciated. As was the mailbox. Despite its lack of use, the mailbox with my name on it, sitting there among all the other very French sounding names, did confer an additional sort of legitimacy about my life in Paris. Eventually I had two mailboxes. The second was not mine at first. Tex, who had moved into the *chambre de bonne* next to mine, 'owned' it, until the beguiling song of Texas summoned him back home. I was loathed to surrender the room, especially the shower, so with your help, Laura and Sophia and I made it into a darkroom. They were photographers and we saw it as a tool to create and sell work. Rather than let the landlord know we were running a commercial business out of the room, we created yet another organization which was called "LE Word Image Services". The complicated multi-language name was designed to provide a contraction which was the existing surname on the mailbox. We ran a little business out of there for six months or so before one or both left Paris for home. Almost as unfortunate as losing those wonderful friends, I lost also the use of the purpose-built shower stall. I could not afford to keep up the rent on that *chambre de bonne* as well as mine. So, it was back to square one. Back to the fold-down shower on my front door.

30.

He had our Backs

Looking back nearly half a century I realize that Leroy lived in his own world. I don't pretend to understand it now and I wasn't even aware of it then. I was living fast at the time, taking risks and being self-centered. I had little sense of psychology and suffering. Despite all Leroy had lived through he remained kind. I think now that some parts of him had been broken and he had put them back together again, and that made him very strong. He never showed any weakness. He let nobody that I knew get too close to him including us, his staff. Odd as it may sound, his kindness, strength, and solitude were qualities that made me feel that my back was covered.

That is true. Leroy never let us get too close to him on a personal level. We never saw Leroy outside of Chez Haynes, a few times in his apartment. But always to do with work. We never sat down for an extended meal or drink with him, even in the restaurant. He never came to our shows or attended an opening. He rarely talked to us in any depth about his life; bits and pieces escaped in stories or in an emotional response to something. A comment? An event? His demons? It was usually after drinking. Even then, he was guarded. But he was not cold or impersonal. His actions toward us told us that. He certainly knew more about our challenges than we credited him.

Leroy's silent advice was always there, don't get too comfy, son, life's tough and it's not going to get easier. Unlike Manhattan where I had previously lived, Paris, was not menacing. Never did I sense that there were places or *quartiers* where I shouldn't venture.

He knew we would be fine on the street.

Only once during my employment at *Chez Haynes*, soon after I started working as a bartender, did I witness any violence. A drunken client had ordered one more bottle of wine. A waitress brought the bottle over to the table. The man looked at it and shouted, 'I didn't order this shit, go get me the right bottle', and as the waitress turned to fetch a new bottle, the man shoved her from behind, saying *allez, vite!* The waitress fell to the floor. Leroy must have heard the clatter, and despite his size and weight, he moved fast, helping the waitress up from the floor. The client stood up from his chair to confront Leroy, and Leroy grabbed him by the lapels of his jacket, lifted him off his chair, and threw him out the door and onto the sidewalk.

Roughhouse Haynes. That was Leroy's college football name.

The clients at the other tables clapped. Leroy hadn't said a word. He walked back into the kitchen. Oh yes, we felt safe at *Chez Haynes.*

He had our backs. Sometimes in unexpected ways. One day I received a phone call from a Radio France producer asking me if I would be interested in reading a French translation of a Charles Bukowski poem for a radio arts program. They were looking for someone who spoke French with a pronounced American accent, and I guess my Canadian accent was close enough. When I asked them how they found me, they said Leroy had given my name to them. Leroy was their first choice. Given Bukowski's grit laden voice, Leroy would have been fantastic. When he turned it down, they asked him for a recommendation, and he gave them my name. They were offering money. I immediately agreed; speaking in my "under the mountain" French, which is all I had. I am not sure if that was when they began to wonder if they had made a big mistake. The next day I took the metro over to their studios—Maison de la Radio—in the 16th. I was led up to a modern studio. A room with a single stool and microphone in the middle, facing a glass wall behind which were two or three radio technicians. The producer handed me two Bukowski poems translated into French on a few sheets of loose-leaf paper.

The French have a fascination with Bukowski, he seems to confirm their deep-seated need to equate creativity and self-destruction.

I was given a few minutes to read over the poems before I was asked to begin. I think they also gave me copies of the poems in English so that I would know what I was reading. Which was a good idea. I did not immediately understand the French translation. The producer asked me if I was ready, and I nodded. He left and appeared on the other side of the glass window. It all felt like they were in a bit of a hurry. As I read, I began to see expressions of disquiet, then dismay, on the faces of the technicians. Before I had finished the first poem, the producer returned. I asked him if there was a problem and he told me no one could understand a word in my French accent. (Too American? Too much 'under the mountain'?) We started again and I was a bit better. Eventually he told me that they were only going to use a couple of clips and they had enough material for their program. I was hurried out by an assistant who told me they were taping an interview with Simone de Beauvoir for the same program. Soon after, I think it was the same evening, the program was aired with a few moments of Bukowski, unspeakably massacred by me (sorry Charles), followed by the marvelous intelligence of de Beauvoir (thank you Simone).

Interesting. I knew little about Simone then, only that she had written a seminal book about women and for the women's movement. Later I read quite a lot about her and her behavior during WWII and the German occupation of Paris. Not nice. So, my view of her life and philosophy is jaundiced. Sorry about this.

Why sorry? All our lives are 'jaundiced'. There are 'not nice' episodes about us in these dialogues. Some, between the lines, conveniently omitted or unremembered. But, nevertheless, we are responsible for them. We were lucky that the demands on our character during our time in Paris were not as intense as they would have been for those living during The Occupation. How would we have fared? I suspect Simone did not cover as many backs as she might have. The stakes were nowhere near the same, but Leroy did have our backs. At least from time to time. He even helped me get film work.

Leroy had worked in a number of movies, and in retrospect I think if we had asked him for help, he would have helped us. I was too reticent and, in an odd way, ashamed. He was already helping us so much by keeping us on the payroll.

I was more or less immune to shame back then. Especially when there were a few francs going and nothing to lose. You were always more circumspect. Serious. You had something to lose, a rising reputation—solo shows, even then, in Paris, New York, London. I never directly asked Leroy for help, but I think he liked to help where he could. It was part of who he was. I do not recall all the details of how the film job came along. I think Leroy gave me a name and number to contact. The producers were looking for someone to write the English language dialogue for a French feature film called *Mouton Noir*. The French script was complete and the actors already cast: Jacques Dutronc, Brigitte Fossey and a young Hélène Rollès. Some of the film centered around an American restaurant in Paris which is more than likely why Leroy was contacted. I was asked to write some English dialogue for those scenes. At some point a few days in, the producers had this idea of filming a full English version alongside the French version to tap a potential American audience. I was asked to help with the English version. For a few days, it looked like this could be a big break. But Dutronc was not happy with the idea, and once he started speaking English, it was clear why. His fluency in English rivaled my French version of Bukowski. They immediately scrapped the idea. But I did get a small acting gig: essentially playing myself, an American guy in an American restaurant. Finally, my accent and my everyday wardrobe came in handy. I was given a half dozen lines in the film, even a close-up. I remember going to a cinema on the Champs-Élysées to see a film and my close-up suddenly popped up in a 'coming attraction' sort of trailer. *Mouton Noir* was eventually released to poor reviews. There were some excellent actors, but the film was not. Despite having worked on the set for ten days, my acting and writing contributions in the American Café were never credited. Illegal immigrants got cash and nothing else. Nevertheless, the hard evidence of my work, and me looking like I did back then, is there in moving images for all who care to see. So far just my wife and children. But more importantly, the film shows Paris as it looked in the 70s when we were living it. And that is worth the price of a ticket.

31.

So, this is a Rauschenberg?

One afternoon we went to see a Robert Rauschenberg show which consisted, among other things, of flattened, used, tattered, cardboard boxes stuck to the gallery wall.

I remember those boxes. One box above all. They were in a smaller room off to the side with several of his smaller studies and pieces. The main gallery was exhibiting some of his large fabric hangings.

These were some textile pieces. I never found them interesting. The gallery was empty except for a few young people puffing away at their yellow *papier maïs* cigarettes. Horrendous things, Gitanes, strong tobacco but in vogue because Sartre smoked them, and the artsy-fartsy *intéllo* people smoked them even if it choked them. Real intellectuals smoked in those days. If you didn't have a cigarette stuck in your beak you were not a bona fide intellectual.

I failed the cigarette test badly. I do recall the gallery being a large space with only a few people in it. We looked at the hangings for a few minutes. You gave me a comprehensive summary of who Rauschenberg was, where he came from, his previous work: what was good; what was not; what was bullshit. You knew the details. Then we went into the second room. I have a solid memory of the moments there.

So do I! You looked at the stuff, went up to one of the pieces, when nobody was looking.

The flattened carboard boxes were the most notable objects. Notable in my mind, for what an artist could call art. The sheer confidence. The utter entitlement. It was not the work of a novice. Not because a novice couldn't do it. A guy who could only draw stick figures could do it. I was only vaguely aware of others being there. I was aware of you standing beside me. We were both staring at the crushed box for a minute or so. It looked like a cardboard box (size of a 12-bottle wine box) compacted by someone just stomping on it. I can't remember what the title card said or if there was one.

These cardboard pieces were called the *Egyptian Series.* Don't ask me why.

The cardboard was covered in multiple creases where it had collapsed and been misshaped. It had then been glued to a sheet of plywood and the plywood cut to the flattened dimensions of the box. Easy to hang. Although it was just laid out flat on a table at the time. My memory is that I said to you, 'so this is a Rauschenberg' then I dug my thumb nail deeply into the cardboard and made a crease maybe an inch long. "Now it's a Rauschenberg and Light".

Some more people had walked in. They were the arty types, elegantly dressed, with a touch of grunge, going *oooh* and *aaah*, and Bob this and Bob that. They walked up to the piece you had incised.

After I did it, I was aware of some people standing behind me. I remember hearing a woman's audible gasp which I interpreted as something like the response to someone desecrating the Mona Lisa. I remember saying to you. "I dare anyone to look away for a moment then look back and find the actual mark I made." It had disappeared into the field of crumpled carboard marks and folds and creases.

One of the men, who hadn't seen you denting the cardboard, looked at the work a long time, then bent forward and stared at your mark in the cardboard, and said, 'oh this is so like Bob, isn't it, making such subtle aesthetic choices, a scratch and a crease here and there'. But in my pantheon of 20th century artists Robert Rauschenberg stands out because his work, irreverent and sacrilegious, had given us twenty-year-olds in art school a *joie de vivre*, much needed after the overly-serious, and often pretentious *angst* and depressive work of the Abstract Expressionists. With the exception of de Kooning. Rauschenberg danced wearing roller-skates, sculpted with stuffed chickens, painted with unmarked cans of house paint.

That is good to hear. I did not feel especially uncomfortable about the incident then nor have I since. I have told the story many times and often heard similar gasps to the one behind me on the day. And I have been castigated for it. It has raised many discussions about the nature of art. Given that I subsequently learned that Rauschenberg had himself erased a Willem de Kooning drawing and exhibited it as an almost blank piece of paper, I feel less affronted by my younger self. Not that I knew any of that at the time. And Rauschenberg did get de Kooning's permission. And credited him in the title. I have never requested any credit for my contribution. Maybe I should.

We walked out of the gallery, and I laughed and said, 'I'm sure Bob wouldn't give a shit, and like any self-respecting Dadaist, he'd probably say you made it better'.

I did make it better. But one would have to have a highly trained and advanced artistic eye to fully understand how.

What makes it better? Nothing. The Dadaists didn't believe in any criteria. Prophetic. Today anything goes, as we well know. You, my friend, made it different, and that's fine, okay, good, terrific. Cutting my canvas at the customs office was pure Dadaism. Maybe Bob would have burned a few of his pieces, given them some color, you know that brilliant color spectrum you get from blackened cardboard. That's Dada too.

A year or two later, I was reminded of this experience of cardboard art, when we took off to Lyon for a few days. We were invited to take *Black to Black* to the *Symposium International de Performance*, in Lyon. And they were providing some financing. My memory is that the performances were in a wide array of different spaces throughout a large industrial building. We attended many events including a naked man trapped in a glass cube. His performance consisted of smashing his way out, through what quickly became a web of lethal shards of glass. It took him about 20 minutes to exit, by which time he was covered in his own blood. The most memorable event for me (possibly not for the right reasons) was the artist from Montreal. We ran into him at a large stage door exit. His performance consisted of taking a twin bed on wheels (furnished with pillow and blanket) out for a walk. On the bed was a single very large white cube, painted with black dots so it looked like a single giant die. He told us he was about to start pulling the bed on an eight-hour journey through the streets of Lyon. As you know, a bed in French is *lit* and a die is *dé*. He was taking '*lit dé*', a pun on the word '*l'idée*' (the idea), to the people of Lyon. As far as I could gather from talking to him, that was it: he was taking the proverbial horse to water. Or water to horse? Nothing more. That is art.

If some museum pays a million bucks for it, you bet. Suddenly it'll be in the art history books and your kids would have had to memorize the date and title for their final exam in art history survey courses. You think dripping paint on a canvas *à la* Pollock is much different? I don't. Or spending your entire life painting black canvases? And then the state hires you as a professor at a whopping salary because you're well known, to teach gullible students to do black canvases. That's not only unfair and boring, but unethical too. The young students will swallow anything, especially in fine art. I would say modern art since the Bauhaus is a huge Ponzi scheme. Will it collapse in our lifetime? I doubt it.

Whether or not the citizens of Lyon ever swallowed 'the idea', is anyone's guess. I still refer to art I find 'suspect', like a crushed cardboard box or a totally black canvas, as simply '*lit dé*'. But part of me liked the bed-die piece. It clicked for a short moment as he left the building. Who am I to criticize? I have many of my own '*lit dés*' to defend. Not the least of which is a wayward thumbnail impression.

32.

Being and Nothingness

I'M GOING TO TALK ABOUT photos again because they were proof of something. I won't say evidence of being alive, but close to that.

For you, it is not a stretch to say it was the difference between being and nothingness.

Sort of, yes. There were photo booths in some metro stations. They were cheap too, five francs, wasn't it? For four photos.

Yes, it was five francs. But at the time I would not have said 'cheap'. I did not indulge myself quite as often as you did.

You'd get four prints, either all the same or four different ones. Going into these booths became a habit of mine.

Possibly an addiction?

I think you and I even took a few together.

Many times.

I also took a few photos with the staff at *Chez Haynes*. I did photo booths on impulse, though. 'Oh, there's a photo booth, I haven't taken a shot of myself for a few weeks, I'll go in now' as if to prove to myself I was here, alive and kicking in Paris. I saved these photos in a Manila envelope. Time passing was captured in those brown envelopes, a prized possession of mine.

I recall you always taking photos of yourself in these photo booths, often with staff and friends from the restaurant. Or with whoever happened to be with you at the time. Whenever we were on the metro together, changing metro lines or exiting, you would see a booth and suddenly track straight toward it. A compulsion. In hindsight, it was a bit strange, given we had access to your darkroom. But the instant response of the booth was pleasing in an existential way. And we had fun, jumping in and out of the booth, sometimes making faces, while waiting for the four distinct flashes to pop. I still come across one or two of them lurking in my papers and mementos from those days. I may have teased you for your fixation on it, but I don't remember questioning it. I thought you were using some of them as studies for the larger self-type portraits of the photo-paintings you were making at the time: I remember titles like *Portrait-Paysage, Portrait-Saut, Portrait-Triptych, Portrait Decoupé*. I still remember the stark, black and white intensity of the paintings, many situated in empty rooms with just a chair or projection on the wall. Excellent stuff, '*formidable*' or '*vachement chouette*' as the French would say back then.

The relationship between the photo booth pictures and my photo-canvases was philosophically intimate. By that I mean that both seemed more real to me than oil self-portraits. Maybe because the photos were a chemical result, scientific, atomic even. I played a smaller role technically with those results than when I painted a self-portrait. With the photos I was once removed. They were nearly automatic. I pushed a button and presto!

I don't remember exploring the symbolism of the imagery very deeply at the time (not consciously), but it does appear to have permeated much of the work we were doing. Cameras, typewriters, paints, props, photos filling empty spaces and rooms became an ongoing theme. Perhaps that's the same for all artists and writers. Filling the void with something. The two covers which you designed for my poetry books were of completely empty rooms and a large theatrical space of empty chairs. In my plays and in many of your paintings, emptiness was a persistent theme. Words and pictures filled them. The set of *Black to Black* consisted of just a black metal table with no top, a white metal chair with no seat, a camera on a tripod, and a large electric typewriter. The set of *One Day in May* was just a pile of thick ropes and hundreds of rags with which the actors constructed the different spaces they lived in very much alone. The most dramatic empty space that we staged *Black to Black* in was at the Farideh Cadot Galerie; her second space. At 11 Rue du Jura. She called *L'Espace 13*. Maybe because it was in the 13th *arrondissement*. It was an ominous, large, abandoned office or apartment with dark empty rooms which she had rented or was temporarily given to exhibit art and performance pieces beyond the usual paintings and sculptures of her contemporary gallery. It looked like it was on the verge of being torn down. The individual props were in different rooms and the audience followed me around as I performed.

That was a success.

It was a lot of fun. Wonderful to perform. And it worked. But it was also a one-night run. No money: expected or offered. That was pretty much how I defined success back then.

But my show at UNESCO was a disaster.

Disaster? Are you kidding? Two-week run. Large space in a prestigious Paris building. Professional catalogue.

That was the best part of the show. Your catalogue text was so perceptive. As for the actual pieces, it was a great opportunity which I blew. A New York collector had arranged for me to show my work in the big central hall at UNESCO. You helped me assemble some fifteen large pieces—and they were large, two and a half meters high by two meters wide. Each piece consisted of large photos taped together. We pinned the large collages to the wall. UNESCO paid for a small catalogue, and you wrote a wonderful, insightful text. I don't remember the opening, or if there even was one.

Again, I remember an opening. And this memory is very clear and distinct. (So, it meets Descartes's criteria for evidence.) There was a good size opening crowd, wine and cheese, and the usual hubbub you hated. And the pieces all looked great.

What I remember is that in that well-heated space the tape holding some of the photos together softened and the collages came undone, fell to the floor, like crumpled junk.

That happened before the crowd arrived.

We eventually fixed them with staples.

Problem-solving. That's what we did. That is what we were always doing. I remember it being a few hours of panic, but the fix worked. The show looked great. And you have forgotten a further highlight of the show. Along with the 18 large paintings, you also exhibited ten amazing wooden sculptures—ten wood boxes (I remember them looking like crates that whisky bottles or upscale wine had been packed in), each uniquely painted and containing sculptures or collages of rags, paint, wood, and wire. I referred to them as mini ateliers, but they could equally have been seen as abstract set designs or studies for *One Day in May*. That whole UNESCO show resonated with so many of the remarkable materials and images and ideas that grew out of the *Chez Haynes* years: the photos, the rags, the x-rays, the ateliers, the portraits, the exploration of self.

Now I tell myself, live and learn, but at the time I was mortified and ashamed. As to the boxes which were later exhibited at the Gimpel Fils Gallery in London, they were built out of cheap particle board. I arranged balsa wood pieces in them as in a three-dimensional collage. I still have them and still find them beautiful. They were also a nod to David Smith, the American sculptor, and his notion of sculptural drawing-in-air.

So, not a disaster at all. It is amazing what memories our emotions insist we prioritize. Perhaps that is because, all too often we remember through the eyes of our worst critics. Ourselves. But that is not an absolute of our being.

I also remember the surreal scene of that exhibition space between noon and four in the afternoon. On all the couches, and there were plenty of them, were diplomats, all men, stretched out for their siestas, and snoozing and snoring.

Enjoying a little nothingness. It's vastly underrated.

I wondered at the time if I should be incensed or admiring of these well-paid diplomats, on taxpayers' money of course, in thousand-dollar suits, some potbellies protruding, sleeping off their post-lunch fatigue.

The ultimate positive critique. Not just 'I can live with these paintings', but also 'I can sleep with them.' Much better than the faux 'oohs' and 'aaahs' you loathed.

Good point. Maybe that was usual. In hot countries I myself do take siestas. So, I suppose *chacun son vice*, as Talleyrand said.

Siestas, naps, snoozes. They are the ultimate vice. The real stuff of being. Something I am now learning to fully appreciate.

33.

The Call of the Aardvark.

I HAD BROUGHT A SECOND-HAND portable Olivetti typewriter with me from New York. Later, my children used to bang away at it; it was a good toy. An incredible little machine. No upkeep, all I needed to buy once in a long while was a black ribbon for it. Only years later did I appreciate its innovative design. The top came off easily when I needed to scrub clean the letter spokes. It weighed little, and it never let me down, year after year. All this to say that I used it nearly every night after work at the bar. I was a hunt-and-peck typist. I never learned to type fast, the way my children can, their fingers race along their computer keyboards now. My fingers could never keep up with my ideas, but that didn't matter, I wanted the barebones on paper. I would correct and retype later. There were no printers then. To type a final, clean, and edited copy was slow for me, and if I made a mistake, I had to white it out with Tippex, a white fast-drying liquid. And copies? There was carbon paper for that, a sheet of carbon paper between two sheets, and you had to hit the keys hard to make sure the writing appeared on the second sheet.

Tippex and carbon paper were the greatest technological innovations for a generation of writers. In the U.S. Tippex was called White-out which

I liked better. It did what it said: whited out errors and mistakes and left a blank space on which to try again. The amount of that liquid I slopped onto the page was staggering. It was the beginning (and the genius) of the word processor in a tiny bottle. I also fell in love with the type-writer ribbons that had a white-out band on the ribbon. You could backspace and hit the upper part of the ribbon for all those smaller mistakes. Like you I was a two-finger typist, but I got quite fast. I could generally keep up with my thoughts. Or very possibly my thoughts were remarkably slow. More ominously, it might be the case that my fingers trained my thoughts to slow down. I like to think this provided more careful consideration of the material before their appearance on the page, but most likely it meant I lost sundry passages of pure brilliance in the sluggish passage of my fingers. Or was it always pure *merde*? (I hesitate to write that word in English. The truth is a brutal companion.)

What did I write? Poetry. And ideas about painting and sculpture. About art in general. I had a few books on the floor by my bed, maybe four or five. I knew I could always take my writing with me if I had to leave Paris in a hurry. Well, that's not quite true. When I had left the U.S. after art school, I had left in a hurry because I had been drafted. And I did leave everything behind, paintings, sculpture, and writings too—–and even my car.

Even your car? I can understand you abandoning your thoughts, passion and creative work to the capricious violence of the military police, but your car? Passion and art are expendable. But, again, your car? That sounds unforgivable.

And what a car! A Buick Dynamic 88. I bought it for a hundred dollars second-hand in 1967. Power windows, power this and that, and when the speedometer got past 55 mph the Stars and Stripes appeared!

The *Stars and Stripes* appeared!? Where? On Fifth Avenue during a substance inspired tequila night?

The American flag on the speedometer.

The last patriotic straw?

So, yeah, leaving in a hurry was a possibility that remained in the back of my mind for many years.

Until the night the *Tricolor* suddenly appeared driving along the Rue de Réaumur?

That was my world, my view until I had children. I could leave the books behind, much of what I had read was in my head and transportable. Or forgotten too. And the painting? Roll them up and leave them with a friend or in a dumpster.

Unencumbered living was a goal to be applauded. When I finally left my *chambre de bonne* after four years of pure living, I remember being extremely proud that I was able to carry all my possessions in my arms. I had packed them all, everything, into four or five empty wine boxes: clothes, books, memorabilia, and my writing. I couldn't hold them for very long. Maybe a minute. But I could hold them.

My writing was not all in my head, and I kept what I wrote in big, fat envelopes. One of the most important aspects of writing was that I could do it and go it alone, it wasn't teamwork, and I could do it anywhere, and most vital of all--it was cheap. In the worst of cases, all I needed was a ballpoint pen and some paper, even a pencil would do. I can't paint anywhere. There's too much gear. Painting at a basic level, contrary to what most people think, is not cheap. Just walk into any art supply store. Check out the prices of the brushes, the canvas, the tubes of paint. Some of those items cost as much as a pair of shoes, a good pair of shoes, mind you. It's getting to be a rich man's profession.

The basics for writing are cheaper. I could hold them all and my five-box-life in my arms at the same time. But then it would all simply be an exercise in self-entertainment or personal therapy. Somewhere along the line writing requires others. Readers for a start. Even if they are imagined. Then publishers would be a nice touch. Again, even if that is self-publishing.

In art schools nowadays, in the U.S. at least, it seems most kids who go into fine arts--as opposed to computer graphics and what have you--do art as some kind of therapy. Painting as therapy is ridiculous.

Except for those whose lives depend on it.

Antidepressants work better.

I hesitate to comment.

Da Vinci was doing therapy? Oh yeah, he was painting the Mona Lisa for therapy? Because he was gay? No, he was doing a job. Like making a pair of shoes.

I will say that the art trade frequently looks like a scam promising authentic experience, meaning or self-truth through tools simply meant for going about one's trade. We debated these ideas all over town—*Le Paradis Mandarin* near the Odeon, and in the *Chez Haynes* kitchen more than once. I think we came to a partial truce in *Le Trafalgar*. We both felt that there was an imposter lurking at the heart of the myth that sells *Art* and *Literature* as something more than they are.

Scam is a pretty good word, for this feeling of being taken for an art ride with all the verbiage and linguistic pyrotechnics. What one longs for in great art and literature is silence.

Is silence not a form of therapy? But we were skeptical to say the least. Scathing is a better word. One night at a party in Bentley's studio, laughing it up on wine and weed, we dreamt up our own grand therapy parody. We merged the 'authenticity' of the animal world with fashionable therapy crusades of the day, including Primal Scream and Erhard Seminars Training (EST), an expensive self-help rip-off scheme then scamming the civilized world. In our sendup, people came to a retreat to discover the true animal at the core of their being, learned the animal's distinctive call or sound, then would join everyone else to shout out the different roars and snarls, and howls in the 'the barnyard' after which they would be freed of their demons or find their angels. We called it *Lambs of Light* which gave it an added spiritual twist. During the party I dished out animal identities to countless people and a hilarious ruckus of sounds erupted in the corner. It swelled quickly and crazily. My main memory is of Bruce eagerly asking me to identify his 'core' animal. I thought for a moment, then told him he was an aardvark. 'An aardvark. Great', he replied. Then he considered it for a few seconds and asked, 'What does an Aardvark sound like?' I said I had no idea. He was clearly high. We all were. He spent most of the party asking people if they knew what an Aardvark sounded like. We had no smart phones to consult back then. I sometimes worry that many at the party felt the parody was more than just a parody. That art is more than just art. And this when, as you say, art is no more than crafting a fine pair of shoes in a workman's smock or a shabby suit.

When I look at photographs of poor artists in the Paris of the early 20th century, I can't help but ask myself who was paying for the smart suits and starched collars?

I still look at photos of those young artists and writers in the 20s, 30s,

40s, even the 50s with envy. They had a stylish, cool look. I am sure many were patching together their clothes on the cheap just as we did. But they had better fashion norms. We were products of the 60s culture of "liberation". It played havoc with our wardrobe and hair. On the one hand I didn't have to worry about my look, but on the other hand, I looked like someone who didn't worry about how he looked. Like someone who was wildly pursuing the call of the aardvark.

34.

The American Center in Paris

Chez Haynes had a counterpoint, of sorts, in the American Center in Paris. Not only by virtue of it hosting jazz concerts in its heyday a decade earlier, but also because of its focus on experimental theatre, dance, and poetry and its welcoming of young writers and performers. The Center was down on my side of Paris, 261 Boulevard Raspail, not far from the Tour Montparnasse; back then a brand-new monolithic beast (which ended up saving Paris from further skyscraper assault). Like *Chez Haynes*, the Center was in a partial state of decay. It was a beautiful, peeling white, collegiate looking structure that had aged impeccably, which is to say perfect for young artists looking to try out rough and ready, flawed, and blemished ideas. It was friendly and convivial and not the least bit intimidating. There was nothing institutionalized or 'high art' about it. (Very unlike what it became a few years later under its Frank Gehry incarnation in Bercy.) For a few years, it became a local home. Although I have no idea how I stumbled onto the Center—I think through you.

My brother Alex had been named administrative director of the place and he helped us. It was big "in" for us, I don't deny it. Hell, we needed some breaks, just like everybody else, *n'est-ce pas mon ami?*

That sounds right. So, we did have a connection. A good one. And, by then, a bit of an artistic record, plus ideas and energy. We staged both plays—*Black to Black* and later *One Day in May*—in the theatre there. They were also committed to providing a range of arts courses, alongside their language courses. And I was happy to oblige, with my experimental theatre course and Paris metro field trips. There was not a lot of money in it, but I remember having about a dozen students, mainly between twenty and forty-five years of age and all French. My French was never brilliant, but I was quickly able to master the vocabulary and rhythm and intonation of the doings in this context—an experimental theatre class. When I was in class, I almost felt fluent. Of course, we were doing experiments with the use of language, so it was a natural fit where we were all equally way out of our depth. Nevertheless, the students stuck with me.

That was also during my contemporary dance phase. I felt I needed some movement training for my performances. Maybe after seeing Carlson at the Opera? For a while I was into dance, particularly the visual freedom it permitted. At one point I attended a few of Carlson's improvisation workshops at the Opera. I have very little memory of it; other than it connected me to a young French dance troupe – Le Four Solaire - up near where you later lived in the *11ème*. I took a dance course with them and fell deeply in love with one of the instructors. The kind of ephemeral love one can only have for a dancer. I couldn't keep my eyes off her, especially when she danced. Unfortunately, my own gauche dance technique did not reciprocally inspire.

Don't be so hard on yourself and your memories and your body. There could have been a lot of reasons it didn't work out. The stars weren't lined up, or she was a lesbian, or married or a guy in drag. So maybe you were lucky.

It was the kind of love in the moment that fades quickly after the film credits ebb, and the performance comes to a close. Or the dance course ends. Which it did. But it did not curtail my interest in dance. Molly, who directed me in *Black to Black*, started teaching a contemporary dance class at the American Center and asked me to join her. I even taught it a couple of times which was insane. I had no profound background in dance. But by then I had learned the basic moves and exercises and could put a few steps together into an activity. And it doesn't take too many activities before you have an actual piece. You will remember that the original version of *One Day in May* was heavily influenced by dance and not just because we were all in dance leotards painted the same colors and designs as the rags that you had created.

At first, for the stage set, I wanted the actors cum dancers to come on stage naked and proceed to dress with the rags which made up the stage design. I suggested we hide the underwear and bras in the rags. The whole idea was nixed. So much for sexual freedom, eh?

I think we gave the actors the freedom to vote. Sometime during our time at the center, Henry Pillsbury took over as the artistic director of the Center. He and Judith Pisar (who I think was chair of the board) were very strong on inviting some of the most well-known American avant-garde artists, musicians, and writers to perform and conduct workshops at the Center. I especially remember encountering Merce Cunningham, John Cage and Allen Ginsberg at one point of another. I have a vivid recollection of watching John Cage setting up and rehearsing an enhanced performance of snails and/or slugs crawling on branches and leaves or something to that effect. He had placed very tiny and delicate microphones in their aquarium which he had wired up to a then state-of-the-art sound system so that he could play the sounds they made as they chewed or moved around, and then would curate or 'disc jockey' their different noises into a sound performance.

My brother played chess with John Cage and wasn't polite enough to let him win. Cage was not a very good chess player, but he admired Marcel Duchamp who liked chess.

I am sure there could have been a sound composition in the chess moves to rival the journey of the snail. Not that I was immune to the charms of Cage's methods. When Allen Ginsberg visited the Center—around the same time as Cage and Cunningham—he headlined a day long international poetry festival. Dozens of French poets and many from sundry other countries were invited to give readings. I remember being invited (or I inveigled my way into the line-up.) We were permitted one poem each. I performed *One, Two, Three, Point*. It was a short poem (only a few stanzas) about a 'sentence' and I read it out five times. Each time I read it, I did so with a different vowel sound: Ain, Tay, Thray, Paint; Een, Tee, Three, Peent; Own, Toe, Throw, Point etc. It sounded even more bizarre than it looks on paper, but it went over very well. I wasn't carried off in triumph, but the response was more enthusiastic than polite applause. Which was, in any case, in keeping with the tone of the event. It was a festive day with a crowded and enthusiastic audience. Soon after that reading, we 'exhibited' this poem in a shop front art gallery in the 10th *arrondissement*. I have a note that it was called Galerie Bichat. But maybe it was just a gallery space on Rue Bichat. 27 Rue Bichat. I recall it having multiple spaces. There were other artists exhibiting as well. Mainly French, I think. We were given a completely empty space/room which we painted entirely white. We audio-taped the poem on a repeating, rolling tape recording. You took a dozen photographs of me in different poses in my dance leotards, developed them, framed them, and hung them in a straight line at eye level on the three walls of the room. All the while, the tape recorder sat on the floor in the middle of the room repeating the same poem over and over.

I remember this clearly. It was a wonderful dance slash performance. Again, here lack of money played a role. We didn't have video easily available then. We must have filmed it. I have never seen what we filmed, nor have I come across the photos I took. Maybe somewhere I have the negatives in a brown envelope. At moments I imagine our Paris years stuffed in a brown envelope, in a suitcase, in an attic somewhere. Good title, ten years in a brown envelope.

35.

So Much for Philosophy, Eh?

ON SLOW NIGHTS WE ALSO talked philosophy at the bar. Sometimes you and Don would join us from the kitchen.

It would be unlike me to miss a conversation on philosophy. Even if it meant leaving the darker, danker, and deeper intellectual domain of the kitchen sink.

We talked politics too, and as already mentioned, Don was oddly quite far to the right politically, which surprised us repeatedly. We discussed Auschwitz and the atom bomb over Hiroshima and Nagasaki; we talked about the war in Vietnam which had just ended. Everybody had an opinion. About God, suicide, love, death, family, socialism, communism, atheism, sexism, feminism, art, history, poetry, literature, film, plays.

There was always discussion. Everywhere and always. And most of it was civil and good-natured. But the details and finer points would sometimes trip us up. Especially you and me. We would invariably find a raggedy thread of an idea to disagree and debate and raise our voices over. It was our sport; but deep down we were wrangling with more than ideas. Self? The others usually vanished around then. Nevertheless, propelled by a 13F bottle of *Chez Haynes* reserve, we excessively pursued some utterly trivial and inane detail. The wine had long since silenced our brains as it simultaneously urged on our mouths. Which, as everyone knows, is when philosophy is done best. I remember we would get into these marvelous discussions about a new book with a new theory. Koestler's books *Janus* and *The Ghost in the Machine* or Jaynes' *The Origin of Consciousness in the Breakdown of the Bicameral Mind* were published around then. As was Tom Wolfe's *The Painted Word.* And I think Jacques Derrida's book *Writing and Difference* was published in English around then. I remember longish discussions about it with Bruce (of the aardvark story) who I think was in Paris studying with Derrida for a year as part of his doctorate. I can hardly remember the thrust of our arguments now, but it swept up a lot of our restaurant small talk and much of our café big talk.

I remember going with Stephen to one of Derrida's lectures on Plato's *Timeaus.* I didn't understand much. I had read Iris Murdoch's *The Fire and the Sun,* about Plato's fear of artists and poets, but Derrida didn't connect with me, and I had only read his intro to Husserl's *Origins of Geometry* and had a hard time with that too.

Stephen loved philosophy. I remember he and I arguing over Wittgenstein's *Philosophical Investigations* during the rehearsals for *One Day in May*. Well, it wasn't so much an argument as me shouting 'Wittgenstein, what do you know about Wittgenstein?' He was humble enough not to respond, and I was ashamed enough not to continue. Maybe that description is too kind to both of us. Nevertheless, it was a moment we later laughed about on more than one occasion.

I want to add something here which was important later on for me. I'm alluding to Wittgenstein's private language argument which says, in a nutshell, that you can't express private feelings in a public language, which is what language is--public.

In the spirit of civility, I will try not to engage here, other than to say I don't think he said that.

Some private languages exist, as between twins, but I don't count that.

Good, because I think the nub of his argument is that private languages cannot exist. But feelings can.

All this, for me meant that every language, including dance, photography, film, painting, writing, etc., has limits. You can't say what you really want to say. As in this book. Or in painting.

Oddly, I can agree with your conclusion. Although, I am not sure I am saying what I want to say.

Accepting this was a liberation for me.

The novel that thoroughly captured our imagination for a few months was William Wharton's novel *Birdy*; largely for the timely link we had with the author, and the timely link the author had with getting it published. For a while, his story was a touchstone because he lived in Paris, we knew his daughter, the book was a best seller and Wharton (his pen name) was over 50 when it was finally released. I do not recall if I met him, but his daughter, Danielle, was a friend of ours for a time. I think she was friends with one of the waitresses. For my 27th birthday you all arranged a surprise party for me at her family's apartment in Paris. I remember it was your task to get me there without raising my suspicion.

On the corner of Passage Charles Dallery and Rue de Charonne, in the 11th.

Wow. You remember the address? I remember you devised an elaborate ruse which included blindfolding me in the car on the way to the apartment. And it worked! I was completely fooled and surprised.

Your birthday party was a bit later, but I remember that party very well. My son was born the following day!

Yes. My godson. Less of a surprise but of much greater excitement. It was an auspicious twenty-four hours. And it all stimulated more ideas and talk and debate. Wharton symbolized some of the art-type tensions with which we were struggling. Here was a painter who had been writing novels for years but, like most writers, had been unable to publish any of them. Then *Birdy*, so the story went at the time, was discovered in a slush pile of old manuscripts, years after it had been submitted, was published with a major publisher, and became a huge success, with awards, a film adaptation and so on. All the other overlooked novels he had written were then published rather quickly in succession. It was an inspiring story which we were watching as it spilled out. Here was a writer whose personal story suggested that success was always just a flip of the coin away. Of course, he also had talent. Which helps but is not sufficient. *A Confederacy of Dunces* by J. K. Toole also entered our talk around then. It was also just published—eleven years after the author's suicide—mainly because his mother doggedly chased down the literary powers that be; (whose mother does that?) So, it takes talent and good fortune—if you can call suicide good fortune. Which I do not. Nevertheless, as all these events spilled out into our lives, they kindled many a good conversation about art, recognition, and life.

We also talked about our fears and hopes and the little things we liked, like the crackling sound when cutting into a pie crust or standing on a bridge and looking at the bulky barges maneuvering their way up the Seine, against the current.

Or the smile of a new baby the day after a surprise party?

Sometimes at the bar, we'd go on rattling away even as clients came through the door, and Leroy would have to tell us to get back to work.

It was unfair of Leroy to interrupt the colloquium of friends with the squalor of commerce. Even if that commerce kept the friends alive.

And other times, quite rarely though, either during one of those bar conversations or at the dinner table, one of us would break down and cry. Or nearly cry. Did you or I cry? Probably. There were tears brushed away in shame. And there were times when our words caused other tears, tears mixed with a woman's mascara. There were muffled sounds, and the face turned away.

This sounds like a confession.

The reasons for such torments were always about love going south as they say. Later in life, we usually acquire a different and longer perspective.

The sheer exhaustion of love lengthens our horizon.

We thought and talked about other things too, of our parents, our childhood, the good and terrible moments, feeling abandoned, alienated. But at the age we were then, all past difficulties were bearable, we could take it all in, or nearly all in. Love could and would conquer all. Even my feeling of exile. Loving and feeling loved then in our splendor of youth was our fortress against all that had been awful of our past. And when that kind of love broke or disappeared or betrayed me--I broke down. I maybe didn't sob and weep, but I broke. Yes, I broke, and it was the first of many cracks that zigzagged through me, sharp and cutting. In my youth love was enough for all of me and my living; later I, and maybe others too, found nimble excuses for the mistakes and failures. I became adept at trinket psychology and blaming my shortcomings on my past. When one of us broke down, none of us had had any helping words because no words could help. What one needed then and there was for love to come back, to say the breakup wasn't real, he loved her more than ever, she loved him more than ever.

I went through it all in the first four months I was in Paris. A turbulent relationship which thankfully ended quickly. She went onto another man and a child. I got Paris and the maids' rooms. The classic betrayal and end of relationship experience. It happened early on in my stay in Paris, which, in hindsight, was a good thing. I had something to experience, to feel, to reflect on and, I suppose, to write about. Back then writing was not just about writing but living something to write about. Living love and its discontents was top of the list. Not perhaps the richest or most original seam of material, but by far the pushiest and most demanding. And then, afterwards, after the upheaval subsided, came a real sense of reprieve. I would not truly experience love for another six years. The following years were not without their romantic ups and downs with various lovely women, but they were also awash in that exhilarating sense of freedom which I will always associate with those days in Paris.

The manageress would then swoop out from the kitchen and tell us to get a move on. Clients would be arriving at any minute. She'd notice the tears on someone's face and say, 'it'll be okay, you'll see, hon, you look great anyway, the tears make your eyes glassy, like a movie star'. So much for philosophy, eh? That's what I told myself.

Yes, so much for philosophy, indeed.

36.

Patriotism and Passports

Leroy had been in Paris since the early nineteen fifties. I never knew if he acquired French citizenship, which wasn't that easy, as I found out years later. Becoming legally French was a long and labyrinthine process, a bureaucratic nightmare. But Leroy had the social connections to cut through the red tape for his French citizenship. You'd think that a country that prided itself as a *terre d'accueil* and on its charter of *les droits de l'homme* would make it a little easier to become a French citizen. Years later, I discovered that renewing my residence permit every year, or later, every ten years, was a Damocles sword over my life. The French could throw me out at any minute.

I always felt the simple *visitor's* stamp on my passport gave me just enough right to live in Paris until the next *visitor's* stamp. I never contemplated the idea of citizenship or even having a *carte de travail.* My existence in Paris was so peripheral to the mainstream, that I was unable to recognize what an official card of any kind would confer on me. As you indicate, it would have entailed a whole host of obligations which, at the time, I was not ready or capable of shouldering. Even my eventual *carte de séjour* was more like a badge of honor. I cannot remember showing it to any official or using it for any substantive reason. It did not change my life in Paris in any meaningful way. A few years later European citizenship would become important to me which was solved when I obtained British citizenship; only to be lost thirty years later in fit of pique or stupidity or both, when Britain decided peripheral existence was the way to go.

Did Leroy think of himself as American? He only hired Americans. Is that right?

I always assumed Leroy had obtained his French citizenship. He married a French woman and was part of the French music and cinematic and culinary scene. But maybe not. If not, it was not because he felt an allegiance to America. I will always remember his remark: 'Baby, I was never American', and the look in his eyes, the tone of his voice, the fusion of sadness and rage in both, as he said it. He did hire lots of Americans, but he was an equal opportunity employer. There was me from Canada, the manageress from Norway, the next manageress from England, the waitress from Australia, the waitress from Ireland, the cleaner from Spain and so on. We did live under the Damocles sword of Leroy's impetuosity, volatility, and the fear of sudden termination, but the firings were rare, and often deserved or came with useful experience tucked into them. There was never prejudice in them. He was not an ideologue, always a pragmatist. He was open to all. Certainly, to all who spoke some facsimile of English and were willing to work for 10F per hour and forsake all other benefits except a sumptuous dinner.

Leroy knew about me being a draft dodger, and though he was an ex-army man, he never held it against me. Was he a patriot? In some ways probably. But he told us that he'd never go back to the U.S. He could never live there again.

Could you live there again? I finally did. Chicago. For fifteen years. But I did not want to stay. At one point you tried. Boston. But it did not last.

Was I a patriot? Am I a patriot? The answer is no.

There is something about the word 'patriot' that annoys me. The part which gives up the pursuit of independent thought.

It does not mean I am a pacifist. Some things are worth fighting and dying for. It was worth going to war against Hitler because of the cruelty, bestiality, and planned exterminations of his regime. Fighting in Vietnam because of American hegemonic hubris? No. The Americans working at *Chez Haynes*, and many of the Americans I met in Paris were not patriotic; they had chosen to leave the U.S. because they felt there was something dysfunctional about the U.S., even back then in the seventies. And yet many Americans, including myself, felt American in the sense that we retained a certain optimistic naïveté about society, a can-do mentality, we could change things for the better. I don't love any country—–that's too big and abstract, it's like saying you'll die for equilateral triangles.

Wait! Who wouldn't die for a good equilateral triangle? Have you ever read the book *Flatland*?

I may love a parcel of land, a city block, a coastline in Mallorca, but to love a whole country, that leads to jingoism.

'My country right or wrong' was never a slogan either of us could get behind. If we couldn't tolerate it in ourselves, we were hardly going to a blindly support it because we had paperwork which allowed us to live and work and come and go on land which, let's face it, we stole from other people long ago. Although there were some exceptions. I remember you often saying that you would always support your children, no matter what. You were emphatic. But then you paused and added, "unless they were fascists". Which was hard to argue with.

One could say that we youngsters working at *Chez Haynes* embodied different facets of America, each reflecting their bit of that nation. And even more than that, we reflected an era too, and of course, we were not aware of it. Whatever America might be, our passports were necessary, even precious. This was before the European Union, when a U.S. or Canadian passport allowed you to travel pretty much anywhere in the world without the hassle of applying for a visa. Sadly, I didn't have the money to travel much. But there were some paintings, where a background landscape, behind some drapery, a room, were like countries for me, even a home. I could always go and have coffee in *Phillies*, that diner in Edward Hopper's *The Nighthawks,* or lose myself in the jewel-like landscapes behind Da Vinci's *Saint John the Baptist*. These places didn't ask for anything, no passports, no money.

The paintings did not ask for money. But the institutions housing them often did. Neither the Louvre nor the Art Institute of Chicago are free. Although the Louvre is still free for those under 26. I think it was then as well. So, I could enter for free. And I did. Many times. Without a passport or confession of patriotism.

37.

A World of Rags

SOMETIMES IN THE EARLY MORNING I went to the *marché* Saint Pierre, up near Barbès Rochechouart, that's where Boulevard Magenta crosses Barbès. I walked around the chaotic markets under the metro. Makeshift stalls sold all kinds of things, from food to second-hand clothes and baby carriages. It was well known that some of the items on sale were stolen goods. At some tables, cardsharps and dice rollers were making speedy bets and keeping an eye out for the police. There were brothels in plain sight, you could see men in work clothes queuing up outside on the sidewalk. It was a sad sight.

These were the same 'sights' that made Paris so 'picturesque'; an aesthetic of sadness stitched together with poverty and tears; suffering and despair; resilience and grim smiles. I like to think the threads that connected them to the city bore more than a fragment of delight.

A little farther west was the Marché Saint Pierre where they sold all kinds of cloth, including canvas, lace, burlap, silks, satins, velvets, vinyl cloths of all sorts. The market was in a five-story building with no elevator. Every floor specialized in a type of fabric. Each saleswoman held a wooden meter stick while she stood by the tables on which there were hundreds of bolts of cloth. I would touch the canvases, feel the texture and tightness of the weave. I would tell the lady how many meters I wanted, and with fast, acrobatic movements of her arms she flipped the bolts back and forth, as if she were juggling, and unrolled the cloth, cut it, and folded it up. I paid at the cashier who sat in a cage in the center of the floor. Later, when we were working on your second play, *One Day in May*, I looked for other places that sold rags with which to build your stage set.

Every time I worked on stage with those rags, they carried the visceral senses of feel and touch and movement which you describe here. And the smell. Mixed with the paint you dripped and splashed on them.

After asking around, I discovered the world of rag pickers, *chiffoniers*, on the outskirts of Paris. It was a marginal world, run by hard-working and tough-looking men and women. They collected the rags from the trash cans and textile dumps from all over Paris. They sold the rags to factories, restaurants, meat packers, house painters, paper mills, and other professions. The *chiffoniers* worked out of immense hangars. The people asked no questions. I told them I was building a set for a play in a theatre. A real theatre, they asked. Yes. And they said sure, take your pick. In these gigantic spaces there were two- or three-meter-high mounds of cloth, torn and cut. The piles were of different colors and patterns. Women were sitting at tables, cutting off buttons and zippers, and throwing them in tin boxes. So, I dug around these piles, and like a child feasting on goodies, I sunk my hand into these rag mountains and took armfuls of white rags, so I could splash them with paint. I jammed all the rags into my car, front and back seats. The VW looked like an overstuffed pillow.

The sheer volume of those rags was amazing. They packed your studio. They also filled countless large bags when we started transporting them. I am surprised you were able to get them all into your car.

Some rags flew away. Nowadays the cop would stop me in a minute.

Less so for littering and more for the coming aesthetic assault on unsuspecting audiences.

As I said, the rag folks were a tough bunch, and they made no bones about showing their knives and even a gun. That shocked me.

Certainly, puts an aesthetic assault into perspective.

I am surprised nobody has ever made a documentary about that world. I took the rags back to my *chambre de bonne* studio. With clothes pins I hung as many as I could on strings back and forth. More were on the floor. And spattered them with paint. Different colors. Were you with me then, doing some of the spattering?

Yes, I remember going over to your studio and seeing the rags all over the floor, sagging and drooping everywhere on the lines you had strung up. You handed me some paint and told me to get going with splashes and drips. It soon looked like an outlandish industrial laundry gone amuck. Your paintings of the Rags series do it justice.

The whole painting performance was like a dance. The cloth pieces took a week to dry. They were bright and colorful. And beautiful. The rag stage design costs us very little, not more than a hundred francs. I often thought of these rags later on. We made do with what we could afford.

It was a superb set design. Not only were the ropes and rags visually striking, they also permitted the actors to build unique shapes and environments during the performance, ever changing spaces to augment the play's words and actions. The play was a series of interconnected mono-dialogues—dialogues in which only one side is heard—which gave the actors spatial freedom to explore the characters and their language within an immediate and tactile series of developing and collapsing, growing, and decaying environments of rags. It was also a practical and easy set to transport. It filled the stage for pennies. I remember you insisting that it had to be cheap and trouble free from the very beginning. And it was.

In my own work the actual creative painting was the easiest part. From my first shows on, it was the transport of the pieces that was always an issue. Who would pay for it? So, I made sure the transport of this entire stage set be somehow cheap. If I remember correctly you took the entire stage set stuffed in plastic garbage bags up to Edinburgh. On the train.

Yes, we did take it on the train. And I do not remember any real glitches. Even though there was a cast of five, plus director and stage manager, going up to Edinburgh, the second time was much easier to arrange. But the venue and time slot were not nearly as kind to us. A near midnight closing time, on the geographical fringes of the Fringe, meant lean audiences. And even less media notice or review. One night, in the second act, I was perched up high on the rags and ropes where I could survey the whole auditorium. I could not see anyone. Only the glow of the exit sign. All the seats were empty. We completed the performance, but it felt surreal, very close to insanity. Later, Molly told me there had been one person.

I'll add here that I think the fact that we failed to achieve any significant success anywhere, in poetry or theater or painting or sculpture, critically or financially says something for our idealism and energy.

Maybe. But I think we simply did what we did. The 'wealth and critical renown' version of success that I suspect you are referring to was never the goal of what we were doing. Chasing that kind of success sounds to me much too much like art for identity's sake, shaped by coin and recognition. Would such a gilded outcome have been a welcome by-product of what we were doing? My younger, poorer, and energetic self would have thought so. Even my older self wonders from time to time. But that is not how I would describe success. Not now. And maybe not even then. We were too busy just trying to get something done.

As Beckett says: *Ever tried. Ever failed. No matter. Try again. Fail again. Fail better.*

Good old Beckett. The perfect recipe for moving forward: trying, stumbling, making mistakes, stumbling better—and, as I interpret it now, all of it without complaint. That last bit is the hard part.

You and I were outsiders. We didn't belong to any networks, social or other, to get significant traction.

That is not completely true. When I look back, I am astounded at the communities we engaged with and how many connections we made.

We didn't do the necessary brown-nosing either.

Whatever that means. Some version of selling one's soul.

And most importantly luck wasn't on our side.

Now, that does sound like complaint. Especially as we have both talked about how lucky we were.

Point taken. But this point of view about luck is unpopular with modern cultural historians and arbiters; they haven't been in the culture trenches.

Some may not have been. I suspect many others have been. And in deeper and darker and more dangerous trenches than ours.

Because of bad luck. I believe in luck, bad or good, absolutely. We were lucky as human beings, not as creative people trying to make a meaningful difference.

I will allow this point, but under some protest about the meaning of the term 'meaningful difference' here.

I suppose that what I am trying to say here is that I mistrust culture vultures, and esthetes even more.

This we can agree on. But they are not the ultimate purveyors of 'meaningful difference'? The posthumous voice of eternity has not yet spoken. Seriously, as life and work have gone, I think we have been spoiled by much more than we might have expected was ours to claim. It is amusing now to think that making money in Edinburgh, for example, would have been a serious consideration. Or even impact. Unless high and dreaming way past the gravitational pull of reality. *One Day in May* was experimental theatre, after all. Success, then, was just building a world with rags.

We made our dreams come true with rags.

I still have one of the paintings from your *One Day in May* series of paintings hanging in my home. The painted rags suspended haphazardly from the thick, rough ropes stretched from wall to wall across your studio.

I did a few paintings on the rags theme, but they weren't as good as I had hoped for.

The painting on my wall begs to differ.

The rags were better for a stage. Literally, a world of rags worked better. And the world is a stage.

38.

El día de los muertos

The Day of the Dead, *el día de los muertos, la Toussaint*--and of course, here we go, Halloween--rolled around, and the staff dressed up in costumes.

Yes! Halloween *à la Chez Haynes*! Great night. We threw ourselves into it. Well, a few of the waitresses, if I am to be honest, initiated the idea and organized the costume part. We went along with it, reluctantly to begin with, if I am to be honest a second time. I think I dressed up as a hobo; that was my go-to outfit, soot covered face and Leroy-type trousers. Actually, to be honest yet again, I can't remember what I wore.

We ate a light dinner, and I put on a mask with a skull over my face, and I wore a black tee shirt. I was surprised at how people, men, and women, asked to see my face. Who is this dead bartender? For non-Americans, the dinner, turkeys, yams, sweet potatoes, and the entire ritual were exotic and fun.

There is a photo somewhere. All of us standing together, posed for a color picture. It was blown up and hung on the back wall with the photos of the 'greats' who had come to the restaurant. Many years later, after Leroy had died, I visited the restaurant and was delighted to see that photo was still hanging on the wall. It had met a test of time, or possibly just everyday inertia. Nothing in the restaurant had changed. The spiral columns, the pink walls, table five on its raised platform. I think the Kon-Tiki roof over the bar may have finally fallen and gone its separate way.

For the staff this evening was, above all, a lot of hard work, running back and forth, but the festive atmosphere got to us. I couldn't open wine bottles fast enough. The waitresses opened the bottles at the tables. The manageress had taught us to hold the bottle at a forty-five-degree angle, that way the cork would pop loudly but the champagne stayed in the bottle, and only the air came out, no spilling, no waste. There were, of course, some macho assholes who wanted to spray the bubbly all over the waitresses, but Leroy had made it very clear-- no messing around.

These special American holidays did attract a crowd—and Halloween was as festive an American holiday as there was back then. All in the name of death. In a cool American restaurant with a cook, waiters and waitresses, barman and a dishwasher who all looked and sounded authentically American. We never fully realized how little we were being paid to play the American characters we in fact were. Leroy knew what he was doing. He was an *impresario par excellence*. Even for celebrations of the end of days. Not one of your preferred topics.

My existential questionings had never abated since college. I had always been like that. I was and still am a metaphysical mechanic, tinkering and groping for tangible answers where they are few. I had always battled against philosophical depression and fear of my own end, as I have mentioned.

It is true you were a deeply emotional 'philosopher'. Certainly not a rationalist, nor an empiricist. And not particularly analytic. So, not very American. And not very French, either, despite the latter's claim to giving the world existential angst and post-modernist madness. We used to say we sat between existential angst and middle age crisis. Now, we are well beyond both. On a good day, I call it pre-death rumination. You always seemed to be in some version of that stage.

This feast of celebrating the dead--and death, of course too--was a good jab into my coddled heart, and a solid fuck-you-and-the-nag-you're-riding aimed at the grim reaper. After the clients finally left way past closing time, the entire staff, all rather worse for fatigue and drink, sat down for our own special Halloween dinner.

Without the bags of candies and treats extorted from neighbors under threat of a trick, like when I was a kid. Back then Halloween was a battleground. We soaped windows, let the air out of car tires or put flaming bags of dog-poo on the front steps of those who refused or simply forgot to provide us treats. Of course, some, the goblins said, exacted revenge with razor-blade-laced fruit or, in one urban myth from my childhood, with LSD. That shed a whole new light on Halloween and prepared me for Paris all in one go.

About a month later there was Thanksgiving dinner at *Chez Haynes*, that American Rabelaisian eating binge, but there were no costumes for this evening. Again, the clients had reserved long in advance and, as with Halloween, loved being part of an American tradition.

Same menu but the drink was more serious. If the reserve flowed at Halloween, Mouton Rothschild surfaced at Thanksgiving.

One of us always bought the International Herald Tribune, and we took turns reading Art Buchwald's famous Thanksgiving column out loud and laughing our heads off. It was the same article every year, explaining the origin of Thanksgiving, *Merci Donnant*, to the French and how a certain Miles Standish, *Kilomètres Deboutish*, tried to seduce a particular Priscilla. The column had become a classic among American ex-pats in France. After we left *Chez Haynes*, we went for a last drink at *Le Trafalgar*. We told ourselves it was the last drink to unwind from the evening's bustle, and we too tried in vain to explain to the late-night French drinkers what we had been celebrating. They observed us, happy and drunk, as we explained *capitaine Kilomètres Deboutish* and the massacre of turkeys, *dindes*, in the New World, *le nouveau monde*. One of the French women said, 'and you helped us beat the German *Wehrmacht*, with commanders like *capitaine Deboutish*?

Little did she realize that *capitaine Deboutish* had a legacy of indigenous genocide and massacre of his own to draw upon when facing the Wehrmacht. And, as we drank and laughed and enjoyed the merriment, neither did we. I am sorry to close the chapter on such a shameful note. But it is about *el día de los muertos*; and it needed to be said.

Yes, you're right.

39.

Dreaming of Switzerland

Chez Haynes was closed for Christmas Eve, but not for December 25th. That was a long night too. How did I spend Christmas Eve? I never remembered those religious holidays. For me, they weren't memorable. I had no children, and the 25th in those years was just another day in Paris. When I was a boy in boarding school, that's where I spent the holidays, with a few others who couldn't go home for the holidays; my friends and I rattled around that massive building in the center of Vienna. Later in Paris, I was free, and I had a job and dreams of exhibiting my paintings. That evening, we gave each other small presents when we went to *Chez Haynes*, but to my shame, I can't remember what they were. We probably gave each other books, we all loved books.

Dusty, first edition, self-published books by poets who went before; from Shakespeare and Co. bookstore. That's what I gave. I also remember many gifts exchanged that came in the form of a bottle.

December 31st was also a big night, and at midnight I kissed and hugged the waitresses, the men shook hands or slapped each other on the back, something like that.

Not a kiss, except with one of our Parisian regulars. But surely a hug?

Even the dishwasher deserved a hug. I had taken my wet apron off.

A few clients kissed the waitresses.

And a few waitresses even kissed the dishwasher.

We were all friends and unattached, and that seems unusual in retrospect.

Unusual? How?

I mean by this that we were creative, and dreamers, with hope and vision, and that made for an unusual bond between us. We respected each other but we also felt our quest, whatever it might be, was a solitary one.

I think I understand what you are saying. But dreaming does not have to be done alone.

What would the new year bring? There was a palpable sense of hope among us young people, and a brittle happiness in our laughter. We sang Auld Lang Syne, and I thought of my childhood in Spain and how we ate one grape at every gong of the church bells. Some clients cried. What were we to do to celebrate the New Year after closing time? You suggested we drive to Geneva. We would all pile into my VW beetle and head for the Swiss border.

There was time. I think we had three days off.

To this day, I never understood why you were so glommed on to that Geneva idea. What would we do in Geneva for a whole day or half a day? Where would we stay? And we had no money, even for the gas, let alone for a student hostel or a meal.

I will concede I was very keen about just taking off for a few days and Switzerland was as eccentric a destination as the idea of just taking off for the hell of it was. And I was not the only one. Laura and Sophia—we were all very good friends by then—were also very enthusiastic. We spent many hours one evening trying to persuade you. It was going to be our New Year's holiday. 'Let's just go. Right now,' I said. 'What have we got to lose? It will be an adventure.' At times you almost caved, but there was always something pulling you back from the threshold. It was not because the whole idea was ludicrous or just plain absurd. When did that ever stop us? It did not normally stop you. If anything, that was a major part of the excitement. Let's just see what happens in the mountains. Or on the way. And it wasn't the gas. Small car, four of us, pooling our money. It was a holiday after all. We could splurge a little. At some point, you claimed it would be "boring" which never meant "boring" but hid something else.

Maybe it was your youth in Austria all those years ago. The mountains may not have held much mystery, or significance or excitement. Possibly the reverse. I don't know. We never talked about it that much.

Ever since my boarding school days in Vienna and going on school skiing trips, mountains mean snow and snow means cold. I was cold those four years in Vienna. To this day give me the Mediterranean heat. Maybe I have some kind of vitamin deficiency, but I get cold easily and I hate it. So, the Alps, my friend, were not an attraction for me.

Whereas, the mountains, I confess, held a magical sway over me. They always have, since I read a book about Edward Whymper's tragic climb of the Matterhorn when I was about 10 or 11 years old. A few years before our "almost" trip, I visited Switzerland as part of a gap-year-hitch-hiking journey around Europe. Near the end, I went to Switzerland and took a cable car up the side of a mountain across the valley from Mont Blanc. I found two weeks' work, scraping old paint from alpine windows at a closed-for-the-season ski lodge. The work was tedious, but the air and the view were fantastic. That is as close as I have ever got to Nietzsche's Eternal Recurrence moment. Well, that and a few years ago in a blizzard near the summit of Mount Kilimanjaro. (I told you I liked mountains.) Maybe that same longing was swirling in my mind on that New Year's Eve evening in Paris. As the evening and conversation wore on and our Swiss adventure slid into ancient possibility, we eventually fell back on the old-time holiday favorite, wine and good cheer, the latter holding sway for as long as the former lasted.

Geneva became, for me, a symbol of what was beyond reach. Silly, I know, but I think we all have our own signs for what we missed.

You were thoroughly entrenched in Paris. That is for sure. You rarely left the city, even when you could, unless for a show, an exhibition, a production. And to see family. The world outside was not so much beyond your reach as, possibly, not worth reaching. Except for love and art.

That night, about two hours into the new year, I drove around Paris, dropping some of the staff off at their homes.

Yes, you would leave your *arrondissement*. Given we lived all over Paris, it was a considerate gesture. You were generous that way. Although, in retrospect, you could hardly abandon us to the streets long after the metro had ended for the night. Not on the first day of the year.

I lived near what would later become the Centre Pompidou, but at the time there was only a big hole in the ground. On Boulevard Sebastopol some diehards were still honking their New Year horns. I parked the car, entered my building. I checked the mailbox. Nothing. I climbed the stairs to my third-floor apartment. I flopped down on my mattress and stared at the ceiling until I fell asleep.

I like to think I dreamt about the Matterhorn that night.

The next day I woke up late and after a coffee and a croissant, I strolled down to the Seine and looked at what the *bouqinistes* had for sale. I bought a dog-eared book by André Breton called *Nadja*. A strange book with photographs of a love affair. I never entirely understood it.

And to think you could have been reading in Switzerland, lazily perusing Nietzsche's *The Joyful Wisdom*.

40.

The Ladies from Wichita

SO, TELL ME, MY FRIEND, was *Chez Haynes* Paris or vice versa?

Back to philosophy, eh?

Could that restaurant have been anywhere? I don't think so.

Aside from a month or so when I first arrived in Paris, and a couple of weeks enforced furloughs, my four years of life in Paris coincided precisely with my working at *Chez Haynes*. I was there until the day I left. So, in some critical ways, Paris was *Chez Haynes*. It was a life-support system for living in Paris. It doubled as a supportive network for connecting and expanding into a wide range of what Paris had to offer. But, of course, *Chez Haynes* was not Paris. Just like the Eiffel tower is not Paris; nor is Les Invalides or even the Seine. *Chez Haynes* is like *Les Deux Magots* restaurant, full of Parisian culture and history. Admittedly the latter is still open. But *Chez Haynes* shares a unique place in the culture and history of Paris. Especially for us.

The bar and the dish water were part of my Paris years, tightly bound to that city for me. There was the Faubourg Saint Honoré with expensive stores, there were the back streets around the Bastille, where there were cheap goods to buy for my apartment. There were brothel hotels in Barbes, and the Hotel Crillon on the Place de la Concorde, not far from the American Embassy.

I never spent any time in the hotels of *Barbès*, but I did stay over one night in *L'Hôtel Crillon*. With an attractive friend or acquaintance Bentley introduced me to from New York City. The hotel was all plush historic extravagance on the *Place de la Concorde*. It was certainly a far cry from my *chambre to bonne*, despite the latter's access to the latest in Turkish toilets and fold-out showers on the living room door.

Chez Haynes made the city easy for us in many ways, we lived under the radar. But if I were to give a piece of advice to youngsters who come to Paris, I would say that Paris is tough, a hard place to crack, and the French authorities make it difficult to survive legally if you don't have money--that was the way it was then in the seventies.

I think I have a slightly different perspective. But then I was not looking to 'survive legally'. I barely knew what that meant. To just 'survive' was sufficient, and all the little cracks and recesses and niches of Paris, coupled with the gift of personal freedom embedded in Parisian indifference made life heady enough. I suspect the pervasive use of technology would make it much more difficult to live under the radar today. The 'radar' has become much more sophisticated and threatening. But the curiosity of youth has a way of seeking out and negotiating its own cracks and recesses and niches anew.

Instead of money you need a vision to survive, hope as big as the ocean, and dreams to light up the sky; such states of mind will give you drive and strength to not only survive in Paris, but you will thrive in it. You will chuck aside the many inconveniences like the lack of phones, the third world plumbing, the nasty Parisians, and the incredibly hard language you will never learn well.

The basics are attainable. Communication with Parisians is possible. For all my grumbles, they were excellent teachers. With myriad perspectives on their fabulous city and how to live in it. On good days my emerging grasp of the language would allow me semi-sensible discussion and conversation. And conviviality. And friendships. After four years, I knew that city better than any place I had ever lived. I loved it.

Not even Parisians speak French perfectly, nobody does. If you are lucky enough to wander off the beaten paths and away from the tourist haunts you will find Parisians, usually working people, who will take you as you are, who don't give a damn what your skin color is, where you're from or if you believe in God and can't speak French. Paris has a rough hide; you'll scrape your heart on it. And anger will get the better of you many a day. You'll tell yourself that the Louvre or the Opera or other cultural centers of pilgrimage are all very well, but the cold in your apartment is still very much there.

And the cold in your exchange with the madame selling you a baguette leaves you wondering if you will ever fully understand the city and its people.

Then on a Sunday afternoon, you'll be queuing for the Louvre, and you'll start chatting with a lady from Wichita, Kansas, and she'll ask you all sorts of questions. How do you know so much about Paris? Are you a professor or something like that? And I'll say no I'm a bartender and a painter.

And you realize you have learned all sorts of stuff from Paris and Parisians. Wonderful stuff. Then along the way, for multiple different reasons, it becomes a preoccupation and must be shared. And you realize that Parisians are not half bad people given half a chance. And you start giving half a chance.

Or another day I'll be walking by the Seine, and I'll stop and say half out loud, 'hey you idiot, look at that view over the sparkling golden Dome des Invalides'. And my anger will dissipate, and I'll feel that my life is damn good right then. It sounds banal. Doesn't matter. As I stand by the Seine my anger ebbs and rises. To hell with the phonies and la-dee-da jerks, they're a dime a dozen.

Maybe it sounds banal. But what the hell. You are sharing it with the river. Especially the rough stuff. Then you can forget it for a few days.

And I did forget the inconveniences and haunted the museums, not only the big ones, but the small jewels as well; the Victor Hugo Museum on Place des Vosges where I discovered he was a fine draftsman; the Zadkine Museum, the Bourdelle Museum, and I knew Bourdelle had worked with the Germans during the *occupation*; Museum of the Romantic Life; the Musée Guimet, and others. I couldn't afford the catalogues, but I took notes and drew. On many a Sunday afternoon, I was the only person in these museums. What a luxury! I too was a millionaire and a prince, and in the late afternoon, I would wander from the Musée Delacroix on the Place Furstenberg to the Rue de la Huchette and buy a hot merguez and half a baguette from a street vendor. And *pommes frites* too.

All the while learning, taking it in. And then sharing. In some way. To someone. Thank God for the ladies from Wichita.

41.

Ashes in the Columbarium

THE *CHEZ HAYNES* YEARS WERE forty-five years ago. That's nearly half a century. We all had dreams, the waitresses and you and I. And we all had vague plans, and we pursued them in Europe and later in America. Most of us went back to the U.S.

Neither of us did. For good or bad we both stayed abroad, even added extra nationalities to our resumes. Although, I am now back in Canada after 45 years.

We continued our lives as painters, filmmakers, writers, some of us became professors or founded a business. We didn't keep in touch very much, and the post-*Chez Haynes* years passed, and they picked up speed as our lives continued. We all know how time speeds up as we grow older, or should I say as we grow old?

I am not sure what old is anymore. Somewhere along the line it feels like we picked up an extra decade on our ancestors; those of us who have been lucky enough to keep our health. 'Ninety is the new eighty' sort of thing. One thing is for sure, we will all go the way of Leroy irrespective of the luck, lifestyle, location, and laughter which define our lives. Leroy died when he was 72. You are already past that, and I am fast approaching it. Given his lifestyle maybe he was lucky. Certainly, the location and laughter he provided us at the beginning of our working lives was a blessing, although often in disguise.

There is still something shocking to see friends' and lovers' faces after so many years. Time did pass, our faces changed so much, not only like seasons in landscapes but as upheavals and earthquakes and droughts and famines, all visible or intimated in valleys and crags of our faces and bodies.

We did get together—London, Paris, Greece, often in a farmhouse in the French countryside. We saw each other a few dozen times in the first twenty years after I left Paris, but as life moved on perhaps only a half dozen times in the next twenty. But the emails continued to flow.

We always talked about *Chez Haynes* at one moment or another. I sensed I had lived and shared a unique time, with unique people; a time still in my memory, that sings to me.

It is hard to fully catch the spirit of that time. We have tried here, and I think we have captured what can be captured without therapy. I feel good about that as it was amazingly special. The end was always in the cards. Most of the others had left and, for me, London beckoned. A new city. A new place to explore. Up on the top floor of 7 Square de Chatillon, changes were also happening. The two *chambres de bonne* to my left had stood completely empty for the four years I lived there. No one had ever mounted the stairs to see them. Then, one day there was some commotion on the landing and two work men arrived on the top floor, my top floor, appraising and taking measurements. Soon, they were appropriating a large section of the hallway and combining it with the two empty rooms to redevelop them into a fully integrated, relatively luxurious, one bedroom apartment. The writing was on the wall. Along with the bullet holes. (Although many years later when I returned with my wife and children, even the bullet holes were gone.)

My dreams? I fulfilled some of them, but I know by now that I have a somber side. I dreamt of many things; most were impossible to achieve. That's the way I am.

That's the way dreams are. They would not be dreams if they were all fulfilled. And while not exactly a dream, we finally finished this memoir.

Yet, these dialogues mean a lot to me. I didn't expect they would give me such a renewed *rage de vivre.*

I thoroughly agree. I have genuinely enjoyed rediscovering this time and these events in our lives. Even if what I learned about myself was not always welcome. That I enjoy mischief and jokes, for example, I think I knew, but in review there is a darker, unkind, side to the pursuit of laughter. That is sad in retrospect, even if the sadness is engulfed in the joy of so many good things that happened along the way.

The best two things that have happened to me are my two children. They taught me to love, and I have felt loved, truly loved by them.

I would agree. The love of children is an excellent remedy for the somber and the sad.

I should speak about Leroy's death. He never discussed his dreams and ambitions with me. The staff and we were aware that he had lived a full life. I just knew of his soldiering in WWII, his acting career in a few French movies, his unfinished book, his love affairs, his fame as a restaurateur.

His laughter. His generosity. His stories. When I think of him now, I mainly have this memory of me standing back from the sink to take a break from the dishes, and looking to my right down the hall, past the salad and espresso stations, and there he is sitting on his stool looking down, peeling potatoes or onions. It's a humble image. He looks deep in thought, deep in many thoughts, full of an amazing life and all that it hurled his way. Much of it was not that nice. But often he was smiling.

In fact, I knew little about him. When he was close to death, I had visited him with my wife and Quincy at a hospital near Paris. The room was dark. He didn't recognize us. I remember he asked for some fruit, and we peeled an orange and fed it to him like you feed a baby.

I remember speaking with you at the time. You described your visit to the hospital in some detail. When I read what you just wrote I had a memory of being there, but I wasn't there. It was that moving and poignant.

He died soon after, maybe a week later, I forget. He was cremated at Père Lachaise. His ashes were placed in an urn in a little cubby hole in a wall in the columbarium. There were few people there, his ex-wife and the current one, Don the cook, my wife and children, another couple with children, and maybe ten other people. It was shocking. We knew there were hundreds, if not thousands, of people Leroy had helped over the years, and now where were they?

Some gone with him, I suspect. If you live long enough, life ends. Others dispersed to other climes. Many simply forget.

One must pay a yearly fee to keep the ashes in the columbarium. Nobody made the payments after the first ten years. I don't know where Leroy's ashes ended up.

Isn't that how everything ends? A last gesture, a gasp, a stare and then the unknown?

About the authors:

Gregory James Light was born in 1951 in Canada. He lived abroad for 40 years in Paris, London and Chicago before his recent return to Toronto. He is a writer, performance artist and professor. He has published four academic books, numerous academic papers, and four works of poetry and theatre. He holds two passports and almost speaks two languages. He divides his time between Toronto and an island in the Canadian Shield.

For more information, please visit www.gregorylight.com/

Rafael Sinclair Mahdavi was born in 1946 in Mexico of an American mother and an Iranian father. He spent his youth in Mallorca where he was home-schooled by his parents until the age of ten. He then attended European schools and completed his university studies in the U.S. He is a writer and painter, holds multiple passports, and speaks several languages. He divides his time between France and an island in Greece.

For more information, please visit www.rafaelmahdavi.com/

Photo credits

Cover: unknown
Gregory James Light: Margaret Light
Rafael Sinclair Mahdavi: Euphrosyne Doxiadis

Design
Rafael Sinclair Mahdavi
Gregory James Light

www.ingramcontent.com/pod-product-compliance
Ingram Content Group UK Ltd.
Pitfield, Milton Keynes, MK11 3LW, UK
UKHW062311290726
14090UKWH00018B/996